T5-AFU-342

HOW TO ACHIEVE SUCCESS AND HAPPINESS IN BUSINESS

BY GEORGE D. HALSEY

Supervising People

Handbook of Personnel Management

Training Employees

Selecting and Developing First-Line Supervisors

Every man who knows how to read has it in his power to magnify himself, to multiply the ways in which he exists, to make his life full, significant, and interesting.

—ALDOUS HUXLEY

HOW TO ACHIEVE SUCCESS AND HAPPINESS IN BUSINESS

GEORGE D. HALSEY

Lecturer in Management,
University of South Carolina

Formerly
Personnel Officer, Third District, Farm-Credit Administration; General Superintendent, Bloomingdale Brothers; Personnel Director, Woodward & Lothrop; Employment Manager, Cincinnati Milling Machine Company; Director of Vocational Guidance, Atlanta Public Schools

CASTLE BOOKS ★ NEW YORK

LIBRARY OF CONGRESS
CATALOG CARD NUMBER: 62-18275

This edition published by arrangement with PRENTICE-HALL, INC.

PRINTED IN THE UNITED STATES OF AMERICA

40185-B & P

To

MY WIFE and SON

who have done so much

to make my life a happy one.

ACKNOWLEDGMENTS

Some of the material in this book is quoted or adapted from articles by the author which appeared first in the magazines, "Your Life" or "Your Personality," and from the author's books, *Supervising People* and *Handbook of Personnel Management*, published by Harper & Brothers.

CONTENTS

HOW TO ACHIEVE SUCCESS AND HAPPINESS IN BUSINESS

1

WHAT DO *YOU* WANT FROM LIFE?

DURING THE MORE THAN FORTY YEARS THAT I HAVE been, first, a director of vocational guidance, later a personnel director or superintendent in business organizations, and finally (since retirement) a teacher in college, thousands of people, ranging from young high school graduates to presidents, have come to me to discuss their problems and their ambitions.

In almost every case, where some goal was being decided upon, I have asked, "Why do you want to do that, what do you think you will gain?"

And, with only minor variations, the answer has practically always been, "Because I don't know of anything else in which I believe success will bring me greater personal satisfaction and happiness."

Yes, everyone wants to be successful. But thousands of interviews with people seeking success in business, in social and family life, and even in spiritual life, have convinced me that the success we are all striving for is much more than just the achievement of some one specific goal.

Deep within each one of us there is a strong and compelling longing for happiness. Of course, we all do foolish things at times, things which tear down rather than build happiness. *But always, each thing we do is done because, at that moment (foolishly or otherwise), we believe that the action will help to bring happiness.*

What Is True Success?

The dictionary defines success as the attainment of one's desired object or goal.

But is even full attainment of our desired goal always *true* success, the success we all so ardently long for and strive for?

Perhaps the answer can best be found in the stories of the lives of two men, with each of whom I was at one time closely associated.[1]

The Case of David Steele

When I first became acquainted with David Steele, he was the president and principal owner of a large manufacturing company.

I do not know whether it was just because we regularly had lunch at the same time and place or because he knew that I would listen sympathetically, but we did have lunch together quite frequently and he did talk at some length about his troubles.

His most serious concern was that his wife and teen-age children, somehow, "just did not seem to understand his problems."

They were spending money like water and paid no attention to his explanations that we were in a recession and that the money was not coming in as freely as it had formerly.

Also his son had been in trouble with the police several times.

[1] There will be many stories like these about actual people. The main facts will, in each case, be true; but, as a rule, the names will be fictitious and there will be other changes to prevent identification.

And to add even more to his worries, his wife, who was about 15 years younger than he, had become a member of a group composed largely of young actors and musicians, a group about whose ethics my friend had some doubts.

But they had convinced her that she had real talent and that with a little financial help they could put on a successful play in which she would have an important role.

The "little" financial help became a burden to Mr. Steele, whose business had suffered rather serious setbacks. But neither his wife nor his children paid any attention to his pleading that they be less extravagant. To them it was just another one of his periodic "explosions" on this subject.

This time, however, there was real cause for alarm. He was actually about to lose control of his business.

Mr. Steele's life story was not an unusual one. As a young man he had started with the organization in a minor position. He had worked hard and for long hours, had lived in a small attic room, and had saved most of his pay.

He won rather rapid promotion, invested all of his savings in the company and by the time he had reached 40 years of age, had become the president of the company.

He decided then that he wanted social position too, so he wooed and won the hand of the young daughter of a socially prominent, but somewhat impoverished, family.

Although his wife and he did not have too much in common, his money and her family background did gain the social prominence he desired. Or, at least, Mr. and Mrs. David Steele were often mentioned in the press as host and hostess at quite elaborate parties.

But Mr. Steele always felt rather ill at ease at these parties. Then, too, more and more money was needed and, to him, more money came only through longer hours at the shop. This gave Mr. Steele a welcome excuse for not being present at the parties.

It was about this time that I became acquainted with Mr. Steele. And, in spite of his still being rather wealthy, I believe he was the unhappiest person I have ever known.

The Case of Karl Wagner

Karl Wagner never told me the story of his life, quite probably because he didn't feel the need to cry on anyone's shoulder. But I did learn to know him quite well and was told the story of his earlier years by members of the organization who had worked with him much longer than I had.

When I first knew Karl, he was president and a principal stockholder in a company with about 1,500 employees, manufacturing automobile parts. By the way, it seems natural to call him Karl instead of Mr. Wagner because practically everyone in the plant did. And he liked it that way.

But to get back to the story, he started to work as a tool boy in the shop when there were less than 50 employees. As was the case with David Steele, Karl worked hard and saved a large part of his pay.

However, at the urging of his parents, he kept up his membership in the singing society (Sangerbund) in which German people are so often interested.

In this society he met and fell in love with the young lady whom he married when both were still quite young.

She was his partner in everything he did. I was told that no important business or personal decision was ever made without a family council. And in this council the children, too, were included, even when they were quite young.

Of course, the younger children were not included when confidential matters were to be discussed. One example was when they decided to use all of their savings and all they could borrow to buy a controlling interest in the shop. In such cases they waited until the papers were signed before there was a general family council at which each member told what he could do to help.

As the business grew, Karl delegated enough authority and responsibility so that he and Mrs. Wagner could take an active interest in the school activities of young people—especially the singing societies in which they themselves had always been so much interested. Their large home became a music center for the young people of the neighborhood including, of course, their own children.

I lost touch with Karl for a number of years, but recently I learned that his son, Alfred, is now president of the company, and that, like his father, he is much interested in the welfare and education of young people.

Karl Wagner's life was a real success.

Now exactly wherein lies the difference between the life of Karl Wagner and that of David Steele, which, I believe, we must call a failure.

Both, early in life, set goals. Both worked hard and were successful in achieving their goals.

The difference must be largely in how much wisdom was shown in the choice of goals.

The Requirements for True Success

For your life to be truly successful there must be:

First, the careful determination of a life's goal which takes into account: (1) your aptitudes and your likes and dislikes, (2) the value of any special training or experience you may have had, and (3) your need for a normal and wholesome family life and for a reasonable amount of healthful and enjoyable recreation.

Second, an intelligent, conscientious, and persistent effort to attain all parts of this goal.

2

HOW TO SELECT YOUR LIFE'S GOALS WISELY

AMONG THE MOST IMPORTANT DECISIONS YOU WILL ever be called upon to make will be those related to the selection and achievement of all parts of your major life's goal.

It is important to you and to those you love that all of these decisions be made as carefully and as wisely as possible.

You will make mistakes, of course. Everyone does. But the number and seriousness of these mistakes will be greatly reduced if, before making final decisions, you will follow carefully and conscientiously these four steps:

Step 1. Get all the information you can which will be of help to you in choosing your vocational field and in deciding upon the wisdom of any other plan under consideration.

Probably more mistakes are made in every phase of life because of failure to get the facts than from any other cause. And often these facts could have been obtained quite easily.

If you are deciding on a career. First, decide (without detailed analysis, as yet) in what two or three general types of work you believe you could be successful and happy.

Then get all of the information you can about the opportunities and requirements for success in each.

Any good public library will have on its shelves many books which will give you vocational information, and librarians are always glad to assist you in selecting the ones which will be of the most help.

Three books which I have found to be helpful are:

Occupational Outlook Handbook (Washington: U.S. Department of Labor, revised frequently).

This is probably the most comprehensive and up-to-date report on occupations readily available. Reports on approximately 300 occupations are given, covering: nature of work, training and other qualifications, advancement, where employed, employment outlook, earnings and working conditions, and where to go for more information. It is available in many public and college libraries or may be purchased from the U.S. Government Printing Office, Washington 25, D.C.

Career, The Annual Guide to Business Opportunities, published by Career Publications, Inc., 14 West 45th Street, New York 36, N.Y.

Describes the opportunities available in approximately 15 general fields of work and gives detailed information about companies which have vacancies in these fields.

Career Planning by Leonard J. Smith (New York: Harper & Brothers, 1959).

An excellent list of sources of career information, especially concerning professional careers, may be found in the 59-page appendix.

It also pays to talk with men and women in the careers you are investigating. Often they can give you helpful information—both as to the rewards and the unpleasant features—which you may not find in published material.

Considering a change to another organization. Several years ago a capable young executive in a fine old organization of about 3,000 employees received an offer to go with another organization manufacturing the same product. Included in the offer were a salary increase of over 50 percent and a high-sounding title.

Naturally he was flattered. And, since he saw little chance for rapid promotion where he was, he accepted the offer.

Within a month or two he realized that he had made a mistake. It just was not the type of operation in which anyone with his more conservative training could be happy.

He left after one year and it was, as I remember it, about ten years before he was again happily located and climbing upward.

And the sad part of it all was that any one of eight or ten men he knew quite well in the trade association to which his company belonged could have told him what he would be up against.

But, quite frankly, I believe he was so flattered by the offer that he didn't really want to find out anything to make him change his mind.

Are not we all that way sometimes?

Of course, it would be most foolish to turn down an offer just because it seems "too good to be true." But, if you are in the type of work you like and are proud of your organization, be sure to get all the information and advice you can and consider all of it most carefully before you make any change.

I have seen many young men and women come into business organizations and work their way up to responsible positions.

While I have no exact figures, I believe that, on the average, those who were careful in the first place to get into the right work with an organization they could respect and who made no changes, even if promotions sometimes seemed slow, fared much better than those who made several changes in their effort to climb to the top.

Of course there is no fixed rule which will fit all cases. My only advice is to be sure to *look before you leap!*

Planning to go into business for yourself. Here probably more than anywhere else extreme caution is necessary. The percentage of failures is appalling. Fortunately, however, both information and help are more readily available than ever before. Publications on almost every type of small business may be obtained from the Small Business Administration, Washington 25, D.C. And, if you live in a large city, there is probably a local representative who will be glad to talk with you concerning your plans.

Also, there is an excellent chapter on starting a business in the book on managing your personal finances recommended in Chapter 4.

Step 2. Decide carefully whether you have the personal attributes and other qualifications needed for success.

It would, of course, be foolish to be a "timid soul" and never undertake any new venture unless success were absolutely assured. But it would be even more foolish just to dash into a thing which looks alluring without considering carefully the probable requirements for success and whether or not you can meet those requirements.

The accuracy of the self analysis of personal qualifications and the effectiveness of this analysis as an aid in making a wise choice of goals will be greatly increased by a systematic approach such as is described in the paragraphs which follow.

Practically all of the personal attributes and other qualifications in vocational choice may be divided into 17 groups:

1. *Mental—Calculation.* The ability to multiply, divide, add, and subtract rapidly and accurately.

2. *Mental—Scientific.* The ability to analyze and solve problems in such subjects as advanced mathematics, chemistry, physics, etc.

3. *Mental—Literary.* The ability to use good English, to write and to speak in a clear and forceful manner.

4. *Spatial Visualization.* The ability to look at a two-dimensional drawing like a blueprint and to visualize the three-dimensional object the drawing portrays. This is important in engineering and construction work generally.

5. *Mechanical Comprehension.* The ability to understand readily explanations of how various parts of mechanical contrivances work and to follow reasonably complex directions for the assembly and repair of mechanical contrivances.

6. *Manual Skill.* Natural skill with tools; ability to do things with the hands.

7. *Social Aptitude.* The ability to mix well with people of all classes, to make friends naturally and easily.

8. *Persuasiveness.* The ability to influence action by other means than by force or financial incentives.

9. *Commercial Aptitude.* Skill in buying and selling; also business and financial ability generally.

10. *Executive and Organizing Ability.* The ability to organize work, to enlist the help of others in doing it, and to guide them skillfully and tactfully in the carrying out of the responsibilities delegated to them.

11. *Musical Talent.* Ability to play musical instruments, to sing, or a love of and understanding of music.

12. *Artistic Talent.* Skill in sketching, painting, or other artistic activities.

13. *Travel Willingness.* In this should be included not only the present personal willingness to travel, but also, the present and possible future effect much traveling will have on the happiness and welfare of the family.

14. *General Health.* Consider especially the probable ability to withstand conditions which are unavoidable in certain types of work.

15. and 16. *Value of any specialized training or experience you have had* as each is related to probable success in the career indicated in the space at the top of the rating form.

17. *Likes and Dislikes.* These too will be rated according to how much each indicates probable success in the career being studied.

The first step in the endeavor to determine whether you have what is needed for success is to "rate" yourself as accurately as you can on the degree to which you possess the attributes and other qualifications which have been described.

To do this, first prepare two or three typed or handwritten copies of the rating form shown on the next page.

Next, write on each of these, in the space provided, the name of one of the two or three careers in which you believe you might be interested.

Now, using the column headed "Self Rating," rate yourself on the attributes 1 through 14, using the scale: E, Excellent; VG, Very Good; G, Good; AV, About Average; P, Considerably Below Average.

As you rate each of the personal attributes, try to think of things you have actually done which indicate the degree to which you possess the attribute. *What one has done,* if analyzed and evaluated carefully, is usually the best predictor of *what he can do.*

Put the rating of your attributes on all of the forms, because you will want to compare your attributes with the requirements of each career being studied.

Before rating the value of specialized training, experience, and likes and dislikes it would be well to indicate in the column marked "Career Requirements" the probable importance to suc-

COMPARISON OF PERSONAL ATTRIBUTES WITH CAREER REQUIREMENTS		
Career being Studied________________	Self Rating	Career Require-ments
1. Mental—Calculation		
2. Mental—Scientific		
3. Mental—Literary		
4. Spatial Visualization		
5. Mechanical Comprehension		
6. Manual Skill		
7. Social Aptitude		
8. Persuasiveness		
9. Commercial Aptitude		
10. Executive and Organizing Ability		
11. Musical Talent		
12. Artistic Talent		
13. Travel Willingness		
14. General Health		
15. Value of specialized training you have had		
16. Value of experience you have had		
17. Likes and Dislikes (Rated Separately) (a)		
(b)		
(c)		
Over-all rating of how successful and happy you believe you would be in this career.		

cess *in the career being studied* of each of the personal attributes.

The same rating scale may be used as follows: E, considerable development of the attribute is definitely essential to success; VG, important, but not absolutely essential; G, desirable, but not important; AV, would probably have no bearing; P, having this attribute would actually be a handicap.

When this is completed, you are in position to rate the value as related to success in each career of any specialized training and any experience you may have had.

When rating experience, remember that to be significant the experience need not have been in business situations. All of your experience is important, even ventures successfully completed (or failed in) as a child.

Your likes and dislikes should next be rated according to the extent they indicate probable success or failure in the career being studied. And it is important to consider them. For example, if you dislike selling tickets for a charity bazaar as strongly as I do, it is quite probable that selling life insurance would not be your best choice as a career.

Finally, after comparing all of the ratings of your personal attributes, training, experience, and likes and dislikes with the ratings of career requirements, put one rating (from E to P) to indicate your carefully considered opinion of how successful you believe you could be in the career being studied.

If the analysis is being made to decide which of two or more available openings to accept, there should be included in the factors to be considered the location and the general desirability of each company.

Step 3. Decide carefully whether the achievement of success will bring real happiness to those you love and to you.

Look ten or more years ahead. If you do succeed, what will be the demands on you? Will the type of family life you look forward to be possible? Will you be happy? Will those you love be happy?

When I was an engineering student, my fondest ambition was, after graduation, to go to South America and build bridges. I am thankful to say that that ambition was never realized. I certainly would not have been happy for more than a short time because I am the type of person who likes to come home and be with his family every night.

I feel sure your goal is not so foolish as mine was, but think carefully. Will success really bring happiness ten years, twenty years from now?

Step 4. Before reaching any final decision, discuss your plans and ambitions with your wife and children and, when the decision is reached, encourage them to suggest what they can do to help.

Few things, if any, are more important to success than the full and intelligent cooperation of one's family. And there is no better way to be assured of this cooperation than to have family conferences when any important decision is to be made.

Children, even children who are quite young, should be brought into the conference when the matters being discussed are not of too confidential a nature.

Most families will cooperate when they know what is really needed. This is especially true if they have had a part in making the plan and, therefore, a part in the responsibility for its success.

But no one can be expected to cooperate if the first notice of any need for some specific act of cooperation comes in the form of a complaint of lack of cooperation and a somewhat arbitrary order that certain things "must be done."

Following this suggested four-step program carefully would, of course, take considerable time. But a few extra hours spent in trying to reach the wisest possible decision may prevent a lifetime of failure and unhappiness.

3

HOW TO DEVELOP THE QUALITIES IMPORTANT TO SUCCESS

AT ONE TIME I HAD THE PRIVILEGE OF SITTING IN the same office for about four weeks with a man who had worked his way up from a job as messenger to the presidency of a large corporation.

My primary purpose in being there was to become familiar with his methods and policies so that I could serve better as his assistant, but I welcomed the assignment as an excellent opportunity, also, to find the answer to some important questions I had been studying for a long time:

What do the few men and women who climb to the top in business life have which the great majority of people in the same organization do not have? Is it mostly luck and pull as some say, or do they really have something? And, if they do have something most of the rest of us do not have, just what is that "something"?

As I watched my new chief in conferences with other executives, with employees, and with outsiders; as I listened to him dictate answers to difficult letters referred to him; and as I sat in meetings at which he presided, I saw that there were six qualities which stood out in his personality. These qualities were *Thoroughness, Initiative with Judgment, Enthusiasm, Fairness, Tact,* and *Emotional Control.*

And, long before the end of the four weeks, I was thoroughly convinced that the high degree to which he had developed these six qualities was the "something" to which he owed his success.

This, I felt sure, was the answer in his case, but that does not necessarily mean that the same explanation is true for others who have achieved similar success.

So I prepared two lists of names, one of about 25 of the most successful men and women with whom I had been closely associated, and the other of about 25 definitely unsuccessful people whose work and personalities I had had an opportunity to study carefully. Then I compared the two groups by rating each individual on every quality I could think of which might have had a bearing on his or her success, not omitting luck and "pull," and even such non-business abilities as skill in playing golf and bridge.

The same six qualities stood out as being always present and well developed in the personalities of practically every person who had achieved any marked degree of success. And among those who had been unsuccessful there was, in almost every case, a conspicuous lack of development of some one or more of these qualities.

On the list of the less successful were included the names of several men who did, at one time, achieve a considerable degree of success; but who, when the test of the depression came, had failed, and have since been unable to stage a "comeback." In each of these cases there was strong development usually of two of the three qualities, but a definite weakness in one; and that weakness, when the stress came, was what had caused the whole structure to fail.

Several times since then I have prepared new lists of the executives and junior executives I have worked with more recently. And there has been no significant change in the results.

All of this has firmly convinced me that, for any large measure of success—success which endures through hard times as well as good times—there must be an adequate and reasonably well-balanced development of all six qualities. *No quality may safely be neglected.*

Thoroughness

While it is probable that no one of the six qualities is much, if any, more important than are the others, the one quality which I have found more often than any other to be well developed in the personalities of successful men and women, and lacking in those who have failed, is *thoroughness*—especially thoroughness in those things which, to the less successful, seem small and unimportant.

Time and time again I have seen some junior executive come into the office of a senior executive with a recommendation, and have seen that senior executive examine the details and ask questions the junior executive could not answer because he had not taken time to get all of the facts. And they were important questions, questions whose answers often showed the whole recommendation to be unsound. The junior executive would have known this, too, had he taken time to be thorough.

Perhaps the most important single thing I have learned from many years of close association with successful executives is that, in the long run, it takes less time to be thorough and to get your answer right from every viewpoint at the outset than it does to dash through and then often find it necessary to correct some serious mistake resulting from not having taken care of every detail.

Look back to the times when you, yourself, have failed to accomplish something important which you had set out to do. Count how many of these times the failures have really been due, not to lack of knowledge, not to lack of experience or ability, not even to luck; but just to lack of thoroughness on your part, to the overlooking of some small detail.

Yes, the habit of thoroughness deserves first place on the list of qualities essential to success in any business or profession.

Perhaps the best way to form this important habit of thoroughness is just to make up your mind that you will endeavor *always, before you call any job finished* to ask yourself these three simple questions:

Have I been *thorough?*

Have I obtained all the information I need?

Have I taken care of every necessary detail?

It helped me to put these questions under the glass on my desk, near the telephone. When I reached for the phone to ask for an appointment to report on some matter to my chief, or when I started to call a supervisor about something on which I had only half information, I was reminded of the need for thoroughness and often was saved embarrassment.

This exact plan may not be the best for you. It matters little what system you use, the important thing in any attempt to form the habit of thoroughness is to keep yourself reminded. *We all can be thorough;* it takes no particular aptitude or ability, and we all recognize the need for thoroughness. The only thing remaining is *to find some way to keep ourselves reminded.* Any thought and effort you may put into the task of finding the best method for yourself will be well spent.

Initiative with Judgment

I once had a secretary who really had initiative, but . . .

I had very carefully prepared in longhand a rough draft of a memorandum to the president recommending some important changes in our organizational setup, and had asked the secretary to make one original copy only, double space.

When I returned to the office about an hour later the job was neatly done and a *carbon* copy was on my desk.

And this was her explanation:

"I know you asked for an original copy only, but I felt sure you would want a carbon copy for your files. I put the original on the president's desk."

When I am preparing an important letter or report I often include in the rough draft two different wordings of the same recommendation or even two recommendations so I can study them and weed out the less desirable. Both had been done in this rough draft. Fortunately I was able to retrieve it before the president saw it.

My secretary certainly had initiative, but equally certainly was lacking in judgment.

Since then, and that was several years ago, I do not believe I have ever discussed the importance of initiative with any group of executive trainees without adding the words, "with judgment." Initiative without good judgment can cause serious harm.

Initiative is the capacity for assuming responsibility and for starting and doing things, the ability to carry through an undertaking without requiring too detailed supervision. It is that something which causes one man to stand out from the crowd in an emergency. It requires a combination of the four qualities, courage, self-confidence, decisiveness, and a certain degree of constructive inventiveness. *Courage* is that quality of mind which enables one to meet dangers or difficulties with firmness and without wavering. It is not foolhardiness. It does not preclude the exercise of proper caution against taking unnecessary risks. It does not even mean absolute fearlessness. *Self-confidence* is faith in one's own strength or powers; belief in one's ability to accomplish a purpose, to do successfully the job he has undertaken. *Decisiveness* is the quality of deciding finally and without vacillation the questions which arise. *Constructive inventiveness* is the ability to see possibilities for action in a situation and to devise ways to accomplish a desired purpose which have not been used before in the solution of that particular problem.

Perhaps the best way to approach the problem of developing initiative with judgment is to determine what are the principal causes of lack of initiative and of initiative exercised without good judgment.

Four causes stand out: (1) lack of self-confidence, (2) lack of practice in exercising initiative, (3) lack of experience in making judgments, (4) poorly managed personal finances.

Lack of self-confidence. Ignorance and fear are almost synonymous. Virtually everything is simple if we only know all of the facts about it. The skilled electrician works fearlessly and, to the uninitiated observer, almost carelessly with wires and connections that would cause instant death if he were to touch the wrong one; but he has no fear, because he possesses an absolute knowledge of what will be the result of each action. He knows the right thing to do and what he may not do. Knowledge has vanquished fear. So the first step toward self-confidence is: *Know your job.*

Lack of practice in exercising initiative. Perhaps the safest foundation for success in meeting important and serious situations is a background of having dealt successfully with a large number of relatively unimportant situations. Skill in making quick and accurate decisions in important matters, and courage and initiative in carrying out these decisions, can be gained by practice in making and carrying out decisions in less important matters. Practice in "taking the lead" can constantly be had in one's everyday contacts. For example: Find out what entertainment is available (knowledge), and reach your own decision in advance as to what would be an enjoyable thing for your group to do on Saturday afternoon. Then, when the question is asked, come forward promptly with your suggestion. It is surprising to see how soon leadership in more important things will naturally gravitate to the person who takes the lead in smaller things.

Lack of experience in making judgments. It may seem to a person who is in a minor executive position, or possibly not yet an executive at all, that it will be extremely difficult for him to get practice in making judgments; but this is not at all true.

No matter what anyone's position may be, he may form a judgment on anything he wishes.

Of course, it may not be his right to take any action about the matter. But he can reach a decision as to what he would do if he were in charge, and he can check the accuracy of his own judgment by watching actual results and deciding what would have happened had his decision been put into effect. This check should be followed by an analysis of the reasons for any mistakes he may have made. There is no limit to the amount of practice anyone can, in this way, give himself in forming judgments, even on important and complex matters.

There is in this habit an advantage other than just the practice it gives. When someone does ask for an opinion, probably the question will have been considered quietly in advance, and a carefully considered answer can be given rather than a "snap judgment."

Another way even a minor clerk can get practice in making judgments is by regularly asking for information from his supervisor in this manner, "I believe this should be charged to account number 59, shouldn't it?" instead of, "How should this be charged?"

And he should be prepared to give a reason for his recommendations.

Poorly managed personal finances. There are few things which will more completely take away a man's courage, and therefore his initiative, than to have his personal finances in such condition that there is a constant shadow of fear as to just what would be the consequences if he should make an incorrect decision and lose his job. With a sensible person, a substantial savings account will not by any means make him careless as to whether or not he loses his job; but it will remove the cloud of fear and permit normal functioning of the mind. A well-planned personal budget plays an important part in success in business as well as in almost every other thing we do. This is discussed more fully in another chapter.

Developing constructive inventiveness. To a certain extent the possession of this important quality is inborn in a person, but probably not to nearly so great an extent as we often think. It can be developed. If we study any example of the use of an original or ingenious method, we shall find that rarely is the thing we consider original entirely so. It is usually the ingenious application or adaptation of something one has seen or has used in some other type of experience. The person who noted how a large manufacturing shop controlled its stock of small parts so as to know just when it was necessary to start a new order through the process of manufacture might easily find in this system the necessary information to use in the design of a new and ingenious system of stock control for the notions department of a retail store—and vice versa.

We should cultivate the habit of observing how people do things in all lines of work, and asking why. And usually those we ask are glad to tell us if we ask tactfully and show interest. *People like to talk about themselves and their work.*

Enthusiasm

Enthusiasm is defined as "an intense and eager interest in and devotion to a cause, a pursuit, or an ideal."

It is a state of mind that does not surrender readily to difficulties, but overcomes them. There are few other traits more universally possessed by successful executives than enthusiasm and the ability to arouse enthusiasm in others. But the type of enthusiasm necessary is not the pep-and-go variety so often put on just for an occasion. It must be built on a firm foundation.

First, there must be *genuine interest.*

That should be easy, because there is no game or sport in which one may participate for sheer amusement which has more things in it to make it interesting than climbing the success ladder in a modern business. It is intricate, and calls for the best thinking of which anyone is capable. It has variety; no two situations are just alike. It has in it an element of chance and excitement; the outcome of every decision is in the balance. And, finally, it offers a real reward for success.

Next, there must be *knowledge.*

No game can long remain interesting unless one endeavors to learn more and more about it. Anyone who would develop real enthusiasm should endeavor constantly to learn all he can about every phase of his own business and about people.

Finally, there should be *achievement.*

With interest and knowledge will come confidence in one's own ability, and the joy of successful achievement. Genuine enthusiasm will follow as a natural result.

Sometimes young executives, because of their dislike of the "pep-talk" type of enthusiasm, attempt to hide the natural enthusiasm they feel about their work. This is a mistake. Employees should be made to feel the same enthusiasm the leader feels. This, of course, should not be accomplished by the admonition "be enthusiastic," but by building up in the employee those things which have created genuine enthusiasm on the part of the leader: first, *interest;* second, *knowledge;* third, *achievement.*

Fairness

The quality considered most important by the majority of the groups of supervisors with whom I have discussed the subject is *fairness*. It is the only safe foundation for any lasting success.

But most of us feel that we are fair in all our dealings with people and probably would resent any but a high rating on this quality. We might even consider wholly unnecessary any discussion of how best to develop fairness. And in the bigger things, there is little doubt but that we would get and deserve a high rating. We would not tell a deliberate falsehood about some employee either to save ourselves from criticism or to gain a promotion for some friend or relative; we would not deliberately claim personal credit for something someone under our supervision had done, nor are we knowingly guilty of any other major injustices. But when it comes to the little things which really count for so much, do we rate so high?

The actual achievement of fairness takes much more than the wish and intention to be fair.

Do we sometimes criticize an employee for some mistake when a careful inquiry would show that he has not been properly taught, that he is working with poor equipment, or that the light is poor and eyestrain with its resultant fatigue has been the cause? Do we occasionally make careless comments about the ability of a person, comments which may cause others to form adverse judgments, when our opinions are not based on thoughtful analysis of facts? Are we always extremely careful to base all recommendations on a fair and thoughtful measurement of real worth rather than on some chance happening, such as one recent favorable or unfavorable circumstance, an offer of another job, or the skill of the person in asking for an increase? Do we sometimes make promises to employees under our supervision, sincerely intending to keep these promises, but make no follow-up record so as to make sure the promises are kept?

For all of us the answers to most of these questions will, occasionally at least, be "Yes."

It is only by careful and continuous watching to be fair in little things, supposedly unimportant things, that anyone can hope to achieve that high degree of intelligent fairness so necessary for success, especially in supervision. There is no halfway in fairness.

Tact

Most successful men and women possess the ability to win the loyalty and support of those around them by saying and doing those things which give to others, especially to those under their supervision, a feeling that they are playing an important part in whatever is being done. The quality that enables them to do this we call *tact.*

Unfortunately, however, there are some men and women, apparently successful by all the usual standards of measurement, who seem to take delight in riding roughshod over the feelings of others, especially of those in lower positions who dare not show their resentment and who can only squirm and wish for the day when the tables are turned.

But I noticed one thing during the depression years. It was those men and women who had felt it wholly unnecessary even to try to be tactful who lost their jobs as executives in stores and shops and who came, very meekly now, to the employment offices of other organizations *asking for anything that might be offered.*

Thus tact is not only helpful in the achievement of success, it serves also as an important insurance against loss when that which has been achieved is threatened by hard times and business retrenchment.

Learn even to say "No" tactfully.

We were on a through bus headed for Jacksonville, Florida, and had been running on time all afternoon; but, when we reached a junction point a few miles north of Savannah, the driver announced that there would be a brief delay because a connecting bus had not yet arrived and our bus was required to wait for it.

As we waited, one man kept complaining about the delay to everyone who would listen to him, and growing more irate all the while. Finally, when we were just 20 minutes late, he burst forth with this demand:

"Come on, driver, let's get the hell out of here. We are already a half hour late!"

The driver could not go. He was required to wait for the connecting bus; he had no alternative but to refuse the request. What could he say? It had to be something that would both definitely refuse the request and placate the passenger—a difficult problem.

As an interesting test of your own tactfulness, decide *before you look at the driver's answer,* given later, just what you would suggest as the best solution and then see how it compares for both adequacy and tactfulness with the driver's answer.

His answer was, I believe, the most tactful I have ever heard used in any similar situation.

1. It was short—only six words. A person who is angry will not listen to any long explanation.

2. It expressed clearly the driver's desire to comply with the request, even though he could not. In other words, he did not make the mistake of putting himself at the opposite side of an argument.

3. It did not correct the mistake the passenger made as to how late they were. This would have made him still more angry and would have accomplished no good purpose.

4. It did not "chide" the passenger for his lack of considera-

tion for the passengers on the connecting bus. This, too, would have only caused him to become even more angry.

5. It left two doors open—one for further discussion if the passenger really wanted more information as to why the bus could not go on, and the other for a graceful exit with dignity unimpaired (ego not lowered) if he did feel just a little ashamed of his outburst.

Here is the answer: "I sure wish I could, mister."

And in those six words there is a better statement of the most important rule of how to refuse a request tactfully than I could write in six pages.

If, whenever it is necessary to refuse a request, we can always have a sincere, "sure-wish-I-could" feeling and *make that feeling evident to the person we are refusing,* we will have gone a long way toward mastering the art of refusing requests tactfully.

Here are three simple rules which, when applied sincerely and conscientiously, will, in nine cases out of ten, successfully handle the difficult task of saying "No" without causing any feeling of antagonism toward the person who refuses the request or the organization he represents.

First, there should always be a sincere statement of regret:

> I surely wish I *could* admit you to the examination today . . .

This feeling of regret can and should be present *and expressed* even though the request must be refused because of the person's failure to live up to previous agreements or to obvious requirements that must be satisfied before the request can be granted.

Second, unless the request is merely an angry outburst such as that of the irate passenger on the bus, there should be an adequate statement of the reason why the request cannot be granted. This may be brief, if the request is for some small thing, or in considerable detail, if something important is at stake. The example above might have continued:

> . . . but your application was postmarked December 2, and the rule, which I have no authority to change, states that, for admission to the examination given today, applications must be postmarked not later than midnight, November 30.

Here the fault was obviously that of the applicant, because the time limit was printed in boldface type on every announcement of the examination. But even when refusal is made necessary, as in this case, by the other person's neglect, there is no need to say, "*You failed to mail,*" etc. Such statements merely antagonize without serving any useful purpose.

Third, there should, if possible, be a suggestion as to how the person may obtain at least a part of what he wants. The example given might continue:

> There will, however, be another examination on December 15, and, if you will sign this request, I shall be glad to have your application transferred. That will give you another week to practice your typing and so quite possibly get you even a higher grade than you could make if you took the examination today.

Try these three rules, applying them in the exact order given—regret, reason, suggestion—each time you find it necessary to refuse a request. If you are not already using this method, you will be surprised and pleased at the result.

Emotional Control

Threading through all five of the other qualities important to success and, if properly developed, serving as an aid in the steady and consistent exercise of all is the sixth quality on our list, *emotional control.* All too often we climb steadily for months, even for years, toward the achievement of some cherished ambition and then spoil it all by some thoughtless word spoken in a moment of stress, by allowing some small failure to cause us temporarily to lose courage, by letting foolish pride or prejudice unduly influence an important decision, by permitting timidity to keep us from doing the things we know we should and can do.

But emotional control does not mean the elimination or even the complete curbing of our feelings. To control is "to exercise restraining or directing influence over anything." For any large measure of success we must have strong emotions, we must feel deeply. We may even have deep-rooted prejudices which we find impossible to eliminate entirely.

The degree of emotional control is measured not by how strongly a person *feels* on any subject, nor even by the justice and soundness of his feelings, but by how he acts, by the extent to which his feelings are so restrained and directed that his actions are ruled by reason guiding his emotion, by the extent to which he prevents his personal likes and dislikes of people or his personal prejudices from influencing his decisions, by the extent to which he keeps worry of any kind from interfering with his work efficiency, by how calmly and with what good grace he takes well-intentioned criticism, even though not tactfully made, by how little he allows some unpleasant or embarrassing incident to "upset his nerves."

It is not easy to achieve full control of the emotions and it probably never can be done entirely, but, to a large measure, success can be achieved by following the four simple rules that follow:

1. Recognize the importance of emotional control to *your* success and *your* happiness in every phase of living, and make a firm resolution to improve.

2. Start by forming the habit of waiting just a second or two before commenting on any subject. This may occasionally allow someone else to get credit for some bright suggestions of which you, too, had thought, but much more often it will keep you from

saying something which, in just a second or two, you realize would have been better left unsaid. And for this practice to be effective in keeping you from blurting out thoughtless comments in places or at times that will seriously affect your success, it is well in *all* conversation with close friends and at home with your family, as well as in conferences and in talking with your chief and with your employees, to form the habit of asking quickly two questions before you speak: "Is what I am about to say my *considered* opinion?" and "What will be the effect; will what I am about to say accomplish any good purpose?"

Most of us would gain the reputation of being wiser if we said less.

3. When you find yourself getting irritated at *little* things, form the habit of *relaxing physically* and trying to look as if you were not angry or worried. Almost instantly you will cease to be angry—and may even laugh at yourself for letting such a little thing upset you. Try relaxing physically when worried by more serious things also. It will usually reduce the worry at least enough so that you can think clearly and plan calmly to correct the condition that has caused the worry. This is discussed more fully in Chapter 4.

4. Form the habit of trying to look at your troubles in retrospect. An old man once remarked to his son that he had had a great deal of trouble in his life, but that most of it had never happened. Most of the things which have worried each one of us most seriously have somehow or other worked themselves out and have not actually been so serious. When you find yourself continuously worrying about anything, try to realize that this trouble will probably, like the others, turn out to be not so serious. Resolve to try to look at your present worries in retrospect.

As I look again at this list of qualities so important to success —thoroughness, initiative with judgment, enthusiasm, fairness, tact, and emotional control—I am reminded of one of my favorite Bible stories, that of Naaman, the leper. Naaman was an important man with his master, the king of Syria; but he was a leper. Through a little captive girl from Israel, he had learned of Elisha, the prophet, and was told that this man might be able to cure his leprosy. So, with much pomp and ceremony, he went into Samaria expecting that the prophet would, of course, meet him with all the honor due his exalted position. But Elisha merely sent a messenger saying:

"Go and wash in Jordon seven times, and thy flesh shall come again to thee, and thou shalt be clean."

Naaman was angry. Where not the rivers of Damascus better than all the waters of Israel? So he turned and went away in a rage.

Fortunately, one of his servants had the good sense and courage to approach his master with this simple, but wise advice:

"My father, if the prophet had bid thee do some great thing, wouldst thou not have done it? How much rather then, when he saith to thee, Wash and be clean?"

Naaman did wash in the Jordan and the story records that his leprosy was cured.

The six qualities on the list are not "some great thing" you are asked to do. But please believe me when I say that thoughtful and persistent cultivation of these six simple qualities, and not "some great thing," is the fundamental requirement for success in the modern business world and in life generally.

Making the self rating which follows will probably help you in this.

Self Rating on the Qualities Important to Success

For your self rating to be of value to you it must be as accurate and as objective as is possible.

Long experience has shown that the probability of your accomplishing this will be greatly increased if you will follow carefully these four suggestions:

1. *Impersonal.* Try to be as impersonal as you can in rating yourself. Review the evidence as if "yourself" were another person.

2. *Objective.* Rate on the basis of what you have actually done, not what you believe you will do in the future. But the actual experience on which you base your rating need not be in business situations. The qualities you are rating show themselves in almost everything you do.

3. *Fair.* In your effort to be objective, do not be unfair to yourself. Do not hesitate to give yourself a high rating if you believe the "evidence" entitles you to it. A rating with a wide range between the highest and lowest scores is much more helpful in your effort to improve yourself, and is usually nearer the truth, than is one in which the ratings are grouped closely together.

4. *Confidential.* Do not show your rating to anyone. I know from long experience in personnel work that it is practically impossible for anyone to make a truly frank self rating if he knows that anyone else will see it. And this includes even members of your family. It is, of course, highly desirable to discuss some individual quality with someone you believe can help you, but do not, as a rule, show even this person the entire rating.

Rating Scale. Answer each question by writing in the space provided the letter (or letters) which will indicate your carefully considered opinion of the extent to which you actually do the things described in the question. Use the following scale:

E. Excellent, probably better than about nine out of ten people you know.

VG. Very Good, probably better than about three-fourths of the people you know.

G. Good, probably better than about six or seven out of ten people you know.

AV. About equal to the average of the people you know.

P. Rather weak, probably six or seven out of ten people you know are better.

D. Seriously deficient, probably eight or nine out of ten people you know are better.

Making the Rating

The major headings of the rating are the six personal qualities given in this chapter as being important to success. Under each heading are several questions to help you to decide to what extent you possess that quality.

When you finish answering the questions under the first heading, consider these answers carefully and rate yourself on *Thoroughness*. The rating will probably be not far from the average of your answers to the questions.

Continue in the same manner and rate yourself on the remaining qualities.

Thoroughness

To what extent do you usually plan in advance all of the details of any important project you undertake? ______

How conscientiously do you follow the plan after it is made? ______

How regularly do you stop just a second or two before you start even a small undertaking (such as making a minor repair on a plumbing fixture) and ask, "Do I have with me everything I will need?" ______

To what extent do you usually carry through to completion the projects you start? Consider all things you have started such as home study courses, home garden, keeping a diary, planning an improvement in your department, etc? ______

How adequate is your system of making sure that you are reminded of duties and engagements and of promises you have made to do something like considering a raise for some employee at a given date, etc.? ______

How closely do you follow up on all details of the operation of your department to be sure nothing which should be done is overlooked? ______

After considering carefully all of your answers to the questions above, but not necessarily striking an average, how do you rate yourself on *Thoroughness?* [ ]

Initiative with Judgment

To what extent are you resourceful in thinking of and suggesting new and effective means to accomplish any desired purpose? ______

When you are with a group of friends and the question arises as to what is to be done about the evening's entertainment, what to send a sick friend, how to pack something for overseas shipment or some similar matter, to what extent does the group usually listen to and follow your advice? ______

To what extent do you always notice and try to find out the reasons for or purposes served by such things as new and strange-looking devices on electric light poles on your street, no visible marks on your laundry, an unusual tool or fixture in a shop you are visiting, the signal lights on the subway, salesperson putting half the price ticket in a box when you buy a hat? ______

To what extent are you usually quick and positive in your decisions? ______

To what extent do you have courage, after a failure, to admit your part of the mistake and to try again? ______

How do you rate yourself when compared with other people in your department in the number of suggestions you make to your chief for improvement in your department? ______

How successful have you been in improving work methods in work under your supervision? ______

After considering carefully your answers to the questions above, rate yourself on *Initiative with Judgment.* ☐

Enthusiasm

How successful have you been in getting other people enthusiastic about things in which you are interested? Include such things as organizing clubs, increasing attendance at Sunday School, getting people to subscribe to some worthy cause, personal selling of something like life insurance, getting your present employees enthusiastic about production goals or safety. ______

How strongly and deeply enthusiastic do you personally become about causes you believe to be important and worthy of support? ______

To what extent is your enthusiasm of the steady, lasting type rather than the type which "blows hot and cold?" ______

How do you think your associates, from just what they see of you every day, would rate you on enthusiasm? ______

After considering carefully your answers to the questions above, rate yourself on *Enthusiasm.* ☐

Fairness

How careful are you to avoid making snap judgments about people and acting on these judgments? ______

When you do make a promise to do something for a person, how particular are you always to keep the promise? ______

How careful are you to avoid making careless remarks about people which may do them an injustice? ______

How careful, thorough, and conscientious are you in preparing "ratings" of your employees, or making recommendations for promotions? ______

How careful are you always to give credit to the proper person when your chief notices something in your department and commends you for it? ______

How careful are you to get the facts before you form an opinion about responsibility for an error? ______

To what extent do you make all reasonable effort to see that your employees have proper equipment and light so that they can do good work? ______

When you have made some comment about a person which would tend to lower another person's opinion of him and you later find you were in error, how careful are you always to go to the person to whom you have spoken and correct your error? ______

Do you often thoughtlessly blurt out criticism either to or about a person without giving proper thought as to whether or not the criticism is fair? If so, rate yourself low on this question. If seldom or never, rate yourself high. ______

How careful are you to avoid showing your personal likes and dislikes of persons in your department? ______

After considering carefully your answers to the questions above, rate yourself on *Fairness*. [ ]

Tact

How regularly do you *remember* to tell people about things you have read or heard that you know will please them, such as having seen in the paper that a son or daughter has won honors, or that you heard someone make a complimentary remark of some kind? ______

How successful are you in always being able to think of the appropriate thing to say when unfortunate things have happened to people you know? ______

To what extent do your friends and employees come to you to tell you of their personal difficulties and ask your advice and help? ______

To what extent do you make it a point to admit to the persons concerned that you have made a mistake when later developments show that you have been wrong in some opinion you have asserted quite strongly? ______

To what extent do you refrain from following each story someone else tells about something he or a relative has done by telling a story of how you or someone you know has done even better? Think hard before you answer this one. It is a most common failing. ______

After considering carefully your answers to the questions above, rate yourself on *Tact*. ☐

Emotional Control

How regularly do you, before you speak, always consider the consequences of what you are about to say? ______

How fully are you able to keep from getting excited and acting unwisely in emergencies? ______

To what extent do you believe that your judgments about people are entirely free from influence of religious, social, or race prejudice? ______

How often has your temper or other emotional upset caused you to do or say things you later regretted? Include in this your relations with other members of your family and friends as well as with associates in business. Rate yourself low if your answer is "Very often." ______

Are your feelings easily hurt? Rate yourself low if the answer is "Yes." ______

After you have made an important decision, how fully are you able to dismiss it from your mind and not worry about it? ______

When something happens to cause you embarrassment, how completely are you able to keep from worrying about it or brooding over it? ______

Can you take suggestions and instructions without becoming angry, even if not too tactfully given? ______

After considering carefully your answers to the questions above, rate yourself on *Emotional Control.* [ ]

But do not stop here. No matter how good your total score may be, for any large measure of success you need a balanced development.

Choose for first attention, therefore, the quality on which you rated yourself the lowest. Read the chapters in this book and in other books which offer suggestions, and make for yourself a definite written plan for improvement. Follow this plan conscientiously for a few weeks, then work on the quality which was next to the lowest. Continue in this manner on through the list—then start over again.

Self-improvement is a continuous, never-ending effort, but no other investment will pay you bigger dividends in success and happiness.

4

HOW TO KEEP REASONABLY FREE FROM WORRY AND NERVOUS TENSION

PROBABLY MORE PEOPLE DIE EACH YEAR BECAUSE OF worry than are killed by all accidents combined—on the highway, in industrial plants, and in the home.

There can, of course, be no exact, statistical proof of this statement. Seldom, if ever, is worry given on a death certificate as the actual cause of the death.

But this does not make it any less dangerous as a killer. On the contrary, it makes it even more so.

The person who succeeds in getting someone else actually to do the killing, after he has deliberately taken away every means of defense the victim has, is certainly as much a murderer as is the one who fires the shot. And if he does this again and again, using many different "trigger men," but, somehow, always managing himself to escape actual indictment and conviction, he certainly is a much more dangerous killer than is any one of his assisting assassins. *Worry is that kind of a killer.*

Here is our bill of indictment of worry as one of the most dangerous of all killers. And every statement in it is supported by published opinions of well-known psychiatrists, physicians, and university research centers.

Stomach ulcers. There is probably no disease more directly caused by worry than is the stomach ulcer. Worry causes the conditions most likely to cause ulcers. These conditions cause the formation of minor ulcers which heal quickly if the worry does not continue. But continued worry causes ulcers so serious that the stomach may actually become perforated, causing hemorrhages and not infrequently causing death.

Heart disease. Heart disease is the number one killer. No other disease even nearly approaches it in the number of deaths caused. Why is this? There are at least two important reasons.

The first is one which should make us happy. As medical science learns to control one disease after another, the average life span is increased. And more and more people reach the age when the heart just grows tired and ceases to function, and the person dies quietly in his sleep.

But there is no cause for rejoicing in the second reason, which is that heart disease is worry's most effective "trigger man."

Probably the percentage of heart attacks for which worry is directly responsible is smaller than is the percentage of stomach ulcers which are caused by worry, but diseases of the heart and circulatory system kill at least 50 times as many people as do stomach ulcers. So, even if the percentage is smaller, the actual number of deaths as a result of worry-caused diseases of the heart and circulatory system is large—much larger than most of us realize.

Infectious diseases. It is not probable that worry itself actually creates any germs or any virus, but it does so weaken the body's resistance to these that the *real* reason for many cases of infectious diseases of all types is worry. The normal, healthy body probably takes into itself each day many germs which the body's disease-fighting forces destroy without the person being conscious of any danger or even discomfort.

But when fear and worry remain present for long periods of time, these disease-fighting forces are so weakened that the germs get the upper hand.

And in general. Worry can, and all too often does play a part in making more serious practically every illness.

Worry is intimately connected with symptoms of rheumatoid arthritis.

There are frequent instances where overproduction of sugar in the body caused by worry has been followed by diabetes mellitus.

Studies actually show that almost 50 percent of all people seeking medical attention today are suffering from ailments brought about or made worse by such emotional factors as worry, anxiety, or fear.

Also, excessive worry can and frequently does interfere with making sound business decisions.

And we should never fall into the all too common error of thinking that these conditions are not real. Worry, at first, causes temporary upsets in the functioning of one or more organs, upsets which will be corrected almost immediately if worry ceases. But continued worry causes these temporary conditions to develop into real organic disorders which often cause serious trouble, even death.

It is of vital importance to all of us, therefore, that we should make a real effort to banish worry from our lives.

But how can this be done?

Certainly there is need for much more than the giving of advice in the manner of some doctors of a few years ago (I hope none today): "Now all you need is to go down to Florida (or to California or the Maine woods) for a few weeks, *and don't worry about a thing.*"

Nor can any lasting cure be brought about merely by the injection of certain hormones to correct the chemical imbalance caused by worry, important as this therapy may become for temporary relief in serious cases.

But here is a simple and practical four-step program by which the habit of worrying can be practically eliminated.

Step 1. Relax.

The first step is simply to relax every muscle of the body as fully as is possible.

There seems to be some connection between the *feeling* of any emotion and the *physical manifestation* of that emotion. Psychologists disagree as to how complete this relationship is in the case of some emotions, but it is a demonstrable fact that it is practically, if not completely, impossible to worry while the muscles of the body are fully relaxed.

So any attempt to banish active worry should always start with physical relaxation. In fact, so important is complete relaxation in the cure of serious cases of worry-caused illness that one excellent book (*Release from Nervous Tension,* by David H. Fink, M.D., published by Simon and Schuster, 1943) devotes three full chapters to the subject of *how* to relax.

For complete relaxation, it is desirable, of course, to lie down; but this is not absolutely necessary. I have found that I can relax quickly and effectively while sitting in a chair, while standing up, or even while walking. Whenever I undertake to do this, however, I try to make sure that the muscles of my shoulders and arms remain relaxed. These muscles are likely to slip back again and again into a state of tenseness unless checked on from time to time.

There is one other practice which I have followed for several years and have found to be most helpful in accomplishing satisfactory relaxation.

Before I tried this I could never seem to *make* myself relax. I would concentrate on one part of my body and another would become tense. It seemed that I was adding one new thing to worry about rather than eliminating any.

Then one day I decided to try relaxing the muscles of my face. But instead of letting these muscles relax in an unguided fashion, I tried gently to cause my face to assume a quietly happy expression, including an easy (never forced) smile.

It is truly remarkable how all of the other muscles just seem to relax when the muscles of the face are "happy."

So I try relaxing all of my muscles, but especially the muscles of my face, whenever I feel myself beginning to worry about *anything*. I do this no matter where I am or what I am doing. And, as I relax, I always feel my worries slipping away.

And in this relaxed physical and emotional state I find that I can think about my problems calmly and have a greatly increased chance of reaching a satisfactory solution of both personal problems and business problems.

Step 2. Ask for God's guidance and help.

There are times when important decisions as to what course to follow must be made, decisions which, if the wrong course is chosen, may mean failure, unhappiness, and increased worry. To most of us, also, will come times when it seems that everything worthwhile has been swept away, and that there is no possibility of our ever regaining our happiness.

If there were not some way we could secure both the comfort and the guidance needed to see us safely through such difficult times, our happiness would often be seriously and permanently impaired, possibly completely wrecked. *But there is such a way.* And the two conditions which must be met before the fullest use can be made of this help, are quite simple and easy ones.

The first is that we must, ourselves, do all we can to help ourselves. This condition was clearly and forcefully stated in a radio sermon I heard recently. The preacher was the founder of a well-known Christian college. One of his students who, throughout the semester, had been more interested in other things than in studying came to the preacher and said, "I know I have not studied as much as I could have and I have cut classes too often, but you have so frequently told us of the power of prayer that I am going to pray very hard tonight. Don't you think God will help me pass the examination tomorrow?" The answer was, "I am afraid not, for *God will not do for you what he has given you the strength to do for yourself.*"

The second condition is that we must have faith. We all know that lack of faith in a doctor can seriously limit the good he can do for us. The same is true of the help God can give us.

And that poses a real problem for many of us. We all believe in God, it is true; there are very few out-and-out atheists among us. But it just does not seem possible that one God can be interested at the same time in the problems of the many millions of people who must be asking for help at that very moment.

I must admit that my practical, matter-of-fact mind cannot understand how such a thing can be possible. But neither can my mind understand how it can be possible to transmit a constantly moving picture across the country on some kind of a special cable and then through the air for several miles to an aerial above our home. But that does not prevent us from turning on our television and enjoying the programs.

And it would be infinitely more foolish for us to fail to use the help which God has provided just because we do not understand how such individual and personal help can possibly be made available.

I believe we are only on the threshold of knowing what can be the real power of faith in every phase of our lives.

But how can one meet the condition that he must have faith, if his faith is weak?

Here are three suggested steps which many have used successfully: First, they have read about or talked to someone who knew about cases where help had been received and in this way have built up as much faith as they could. Second, they have done all they could themselves. And third, quietly and calmly and in as fully relaxed a condition and position as it was possible to assume, they have asked for help. *And they did receive that help.*

Of course, the help was not always as miraculous as some cases they had read about, *but they did receive help.* And the fact that they had received *some* help enabled them to ask with greater faith the next time, and so full faith came, perhaps gradually, *but it did come.*

Dr. Norman Vincent Peale often calls attention in his sermons and in his books to the faith-building power of repeating again and again, many times throughout the day, appropriate verses from the Bible.

My own experience in doing this has proved so helpful to me that I believe the story of that experience will be interesting and helpful to others.

I tried to find one verse which I could use for most of my problems, and I selected Psalms 25:4. With some slight changes to express in today's language what I believe was the original meaning and with the addition of a request for wisdom and strength, here it is:

> *Show me thy way O Lord; teach me my part. And give me wisdom and strength to do it.*

I chose this simple prayer verse because I believe firmly that God's way is the best way for me to follow in *everything* I do. Through the ages, men and animals who have best adjusted themselves to God's laws have lived and have been happy.

I believe that the more completely *I* can adjust *my* life to God's way, to God's laws, the more truly successful and happy will be *my* life.

I believe too that, if I ask, I will be shown God's way, will be taught what is my part, and will be given the faith, the wisdom, and the strength to do it.

I believe this because again and again it has happened.

For some time now, whenever I feel myself beginning to worry about anything at all, small problems or more serious ones, I have tried to make it a practice: (1) to relax physically as fully as circumstances permit, (2) to close my eyes for a few moments if this is practicable, and (3) whether my eyes are closed or not, to repeat silently several times this simple prayer-verse, "Show me thy way, O Lord; teach me my part. And give me wisdom and strength to do it."

Often at night, when there is some difficult or unpleasant situation which I know must be dealt with the next day, I go to sleep repeating the verse over and over. I say the words in cadence with the ticking of the bedside clock so that the clock will continue saying it with me after I have fallen asleep.

It is almost unbelievable how much and in how many different ways the practice of repeating this verse and prayer has helped me.

But two more steps are necessary if worry and tension are to be successfully banished.

Step 3. Discuss your problem with someone who can help you.

All too often we keep our worries to ourselves. It may be, as it is with so many men, that we feel it to be a sign of weakness to discuss our problems with our wives and children. Our duty as husbands and fathers, we say, is to provide for them and to protect them. And so we lock our worries within ourselves and put on a "brave front." But I might add that we die several years younger than we should and leave our widows with the entire load to carry, often after our financial resources have been sadly depleted by our long illnesses.

No, we are not doing any kindness to those we love and who love us by keeping our worries to ourselves.

Our wives and our children, even children who are quite young, will understand and be glad to help if all along the situations are explained to them calmly and tactfully.

And it is indeed surprising and gratifying how, after we have discussed our problems with someone who is interested in us, tenseness and worry will vanish and how much less formidable the problems will look.

But for a really decisive and lasting victory over worry, one more step must be taken.

Step 4. Lay out and follow a plan which will reduce to a minimum those conditions which may cause worry.

Here too we will need the help of whoever has a part in our activities, our associates in business, our wives or husbands, our children, and, of course, our unseen Partner, whose counsel we should seek frequently.

There is not space in this brief chapter for detailed suggestions on what should be included in the plan. But, since research has shown that more than half of all of the worries of the average family spring from financial difficulties, the plan should, first of all, include a realistic program for living within the available income and saving something for retirement and for unexpected emergencies. The whole family should know the exact situation and have a part in planning and in carrying out the program.

Of course, money does not make happiness. In fact, quite often the opposite is true. But the lack of at least a reasonable degree of financial security often introduces tensions which make it difficult for anyone to be either successful or happy.

Constant fear of almost immediate privation if one should lose his job, driving on poor tires or without insurance because one just cannot afford the cost, dread of what would happen financially if there were a serious illness—all of these and similar things can make it difficult indeed to avoid an almost constant feeling of impending disaster and, unless corrected, may play a large part in bringing on the disaster.

Several good books on the financial problems of the average family may be found in almost any public library. A composite statement of the advice given in these books might be summarized about as follows:

1. Pay as you go. Except in such cases as buying a home or some expensive appliance *which is really needed*, avoid buying on the installment plan. Even then be sure you can meet the necessary payments without too serious a strain.

2. Plan to spend less than you earn.

3. Plan to put a certain amount each pay day into a savings account so as to be prepared to meet unexpected expenses when they occur. If it seems to be impossible for you to save any money for emergencies, there is one important but often neglected truth which should be kept constantly in mind as you plan. It is that there are only two ways to solve that problem: (1) to find a way to increase the family income, or (2) to do without something you probably now consider to be "indispensable." Borrowing to meet anything except the more serious and unpredictable emergency expenses is never a satisfactory solution. And, if borrowing is continued in increasing amounts, it may lead to truly disastrous results.

4. Start a life insurance program as early in your life as possible. Discuss this with the representative of one or more well-

established insurance companies. Choose the plan which will give you and your family the maximum of protection when you need it most.

5. Build job security for yourself by doing just a little more than is demanded of you on your job, and by preparing for promotion. Learn all you can about the business. Attend night classes or take correspondence courses if this will help. Remember that a feeling of reasonable certainty of job security, based on good service rendered to your employer, is one of the most important requirements for freedom from worry.

6. Finally, and this is most important, remember that the person who admits quite frankly that he cannot afford to do certain things that his neighbors may be doing wins their respect much more than does the person who tries to live beyond his means in order to keep up appearances.

Many questions will arise in the application of these suggestions. Several of the more important of these, such as the advantages and disadvantages of checking accounts, installment buying, personal loans, life insurance, annuities, and home ownership are discussed in a most helpful manner in *Managing Personal Finances* by David F. Jordan and Edward F. Willett (Englewood Cliffs, N.J.: Prentice-Hall, Inc., 3rd edition, 1951).

Some suggestions as to how to reduce to a safe minimum some of the other causes of worry are given in the chapters which follow.

But no matter how carefully you follow all of these suggestions, some things are almost certain to happen about which you cannot help but worry. This is natural and normal and should be no cause for alarm. If you have tried conscientiously to banish the more common causes of worry and have enlisted all of the members of your family as partners in the enterprise, worry will be so reduced in frequency and intensity that, when it does come, it can be handled without any serious damage, physical or emotional.

And worry will have become completely impotent as a killer and even as a threat to success and happiness.

Self Rating on Keeping Reasonably Free From Worry

Following the instructions and using the rating scale given at the close of Chapter 3, answer each question by writing in the space provided the letter (or letters) which will indicate your carefully considered opinion of the extent to which you do the things described in the question:

1. To what extent are you able to relax fully, and how regularly do you do this when beginning to worry about anything? ______

2. To what extent do you regularly ask for God's help and guidance when confronted with serious problems? ______

3. To what extent do you regularly discuss your problems with your family? ______

4. To what extent have you "done your part" by doing what you can to reduce to a minimum conditions which cause worry? ______

5. Using all of these helps, how successful have your efforts been to become reasonably free from worry? [ ]

6. If the answer to this question is not what you would like it to be, how do you rate the effort you have made to locate and correct the reason for this? ______

5

HOW TO UNDERSTAND AND INFLUENCE HUMAN BEHAVIOR

Why Do Human Beings Do the Things They Do?

WE KNOW THAT AN ELECTRIC MOTOR WILL NOT RUN until a current of electricity is caused to flow through its coils, and that a steam locomotive will not move until steam is admitted into its cylinders.

Is there some one thing which has the same relationship to human behavior that electricity does to the motion of the electric motor and that steam does to that of the locomotive? If there is, it would be important for us to know what that thing is and to base our technique of influencing people on the fullest possible use of it.

Perhaps if we study some of our simpler actions we may discover a common cause for these, and then we may find that this same cause applies to all of our actions, from the simplest to the most complex.

You buy a magazine because you know that you are to have the evening alone and you want the pleasure which reading gives you. I jump out of the way when an automobile horn sounds because there is a fear that I may get run over if I do not do so. You drop a dollar into a Salvation Army Christmas kettle because you want that inward glow of satisfaction that comes when you have helped someone less fortunate than you.

There are probably several reasons why we go to work each day. There is the elemental want for food and shelter and various comforts which the money we earn by working will enable us to get. And we want the feeling of satisfaction and personal worthwhileness which comes from doing a good job. The sum of these wants is stronger than the want to go to the ball game or to sleep late, so we go to work.

If we examine these and other of any person's everyday decisions and actions, we shall find that at the *beginning* of each and serving as the *cause* of each there was a *want for something* felt by that person. And this will be found to be true of all voluntary human actions. Even fear, which was mentioned once as a cause for action, is a want to avoid some unpleasant happening.

Everything, absolutely everything, you or I or anyone else does is done because, first, there is a want (either for something or to avoid something) and, second, there is a belief (or at least a hope) that to do some certain thing will help to gain that which is wanted.

There can be no voluntary human action except as a result of the person's own wants.

The person's wants may be for comfort or safety, for the satisfaction that comes when he has pleased someone he respects and admires, for the pleasure brought by commendation and applause, or it may be merely the want to avoid something unpleasant, such as being without a job.

But, whatever the person's wants, these will be the primary motivating cause of all of his actions, not the will or the wish of anyone else.

I had reached about this point in a discussion with an evening-school group recently when Mr. Wilson, an older member of the group, raised this question:

"All of this sounds fine, even beautiful, but is it really true in *every* case as things actually happen on the job? A few years ago I worked under a very arbitrary supervisor. One day he told me to arrange my stock in a certain way which I felt sure would make some fast moving items hard to get quickly when customers wanted them. As politely as I knew how, I asked if it might not be better if we put these items nearer to the cash register, because, . . . That was as far as I got. He interrupted with this comment: 'When I want your advice I'll ask for it. I want the stock arranged exactly the way I told you and I am the boss. Do you understand that?'

"I understood all right and I arranged the stock exactly as he directed, *but I surely did not want to do it that way.*

"In that case wasn't it the supervisor's want and not my want that made me arrange my stock in what I knew to be the wrong way?"

"It does sound as if your action was caused by your supervisor's wants, doesn't it, Mr. Wilson?" was my reply. "But let's look a little deeper. If you really *wanted* to arrange your stock in what you knew to be the best way, just why did you do it the way the boss ordered it done?"

"Because I knew he would fire me on the spot if I did not do so.'

"Why did you want to stay if your boss was so unpleasant?"

"I didn't really *want* to stay, but we had recently bought a new home and I knew that if I did not keep up the payments we would lose it."

After some additional discussion the group decided that in this case Mr. Wilson's want to keep the home for his family was stronger than his want to assert his own independence and arrange the stock as he thought it should be, and that *it was this want of his own* which made him comply.

Other members of the group told of cases in which they had, under pressure, done things they did not want to do, but in each case it was decided, after some discussion, that the person's own wants which were satisfied by *doing* the unpleasant thing were stronger than were his wants which would have been satisfied by not doing it, and in every case it was these stronger wants of the person himself which really caused him to do it.

It is important for any one who aspires to success in any endeavor which requires the help of other people to get the full significance of the fact that before there will be any action by any person there must be three conditions present:

1. *The person must feel a want for something or a want to avoid something (a fear). No one will ever do anything at all unless he wants something or fears something.*
2. The person must believe, or at least hope, that some definite thing which he can do will help toward the realization of his want or elimination of the fear.
3. Finally, this belief or hope must remain in the person's consciousness long enough for the appropriate action to take place.

One of the most interesting examples I have ever seen of an attempt to influence action by making sure, step by step, that there were present the three conditions necessary for action is this advertisement which appeared several years ago in the classified section of the *Washington Star:*

> PAYMENTS on your home are made easy by renting a room. Renting a room is made easy by an advertisement in the classified section of the Star. Call District 5800; open until 9:00 P.M.

The advertisement appeared in the days when a large part of the population of Washington was made up of government employees with steady jobs, but low salaries. Many of them were buying their homes with small monthly payments and the want to find some way to make these payments more easily was an ever-present one.

This want is mentioned tactfully and skillfully in the first part of the first sentence:

Payments on your home are made easy . . . . .

Then comes step two, without any break. The definite thing which the reader can do to help toward the satisfaction of his want is told; the reader is also told how easy it is to do that thing:

. . . . *by renting a room. Renting a room is made easy by an advertisement in the classified section of the Star.*

But if the reader must wait until the next morning to place the advertisement and, even then, must walk some blocks to the nearest office of the *Star,* it is possible that he will put off taking care of the matter for a few days—possibly forever. So the third condition necessary to assuring that the desired action will be carried out is taken care of. The reader is shown how simple and easy it is for him to place his advertisement *immediately,* before he can forget about it:

Call District 5800; open until 9:00 P.M.

But let us rewrite the advertisement, putting first the want of the person who writes it.

> THE EDITOR of the Star has asked that the number of classified advertisements in the paper be increased, and I am anxious to make my quota. Don't you have a room you would like to rent? The income would, undoubtedly, be of assistance in meeting the payments on your home. Our office is open every evening until 9:00 o'clock and the telephone number is District 5800.

The difference in appeal is so obvious that no comment is necessary.

Perhaps this will give us the answer to why it is that Hopalong Cassidy and the Lone Ranger have often had so much more influence in causing our children to follow the rules of good health and safety than we parents have had.

The answer is simple—and it is nothing that parents need worry about either. All children want to grow up to be strong and brave like Hopalong and the Lone Ranger. So, when their favorite hero tells them *how to satisfy this want,* they are enthusiastic about following the rules. And they get secret codes and other greatly desired rewards, too.

As parents, supervisors, teachers, salesmen, leaders of voluntary groups, or just as people who wish to cause other people to like us, we can learn much from these admirable gentlemen of radio and television.

If we are to have any real success in influencing the behavior of other people, we should, first, endeavor to understand more fully just what *their* wants are and then to find out how best to enable them to derive as full satisfaction as is possible of these wants *through doing the things we would like to have them do.*

There is definitely no method more effective than this in influencing even the people to whom we feel we have the right to give orders.

And in the leadership of voluntary groups and in getting people to like us, I believe we can go one step further and say that *it is the only method that will ever prove effective.*

Five Steps in Influencing Behavior

Step 1. Decide what wants of the person can best be satisfied by doing what you want done.

Review carefully the likes and dislikes of the person, considering especially those wants and ambitions which are the most important in his life.

It is well here to use a systematic approach. People—all of us —want many things, but when we examine all of these things we shall find that all of our wants are related to and spring from one or more of five fundamental wants, which are:

1. To feel more important, more worthy, more worthwhile.
2. To live safely, securely, and comfortably.
3. To find the right mate and rear a family.
4. To explore the unknown.
5. Occasionally to forget the cares and problems of life and to play or to be entertained.

We shall be more thorough in considering all of the person's wants and probably more effective in selecting those wants which will be the most helpful to us in securing cooperation, if we review separately the wants related to each of these five fundamental wants.

To feel more important, more worthy, more worthwhile. We can at the outset be sure that this want is present, because practically every person wants more strongly than he wants any other one thing to have and to hold some feeling of personal importance, of self-esteem; to be able to compare himself with his associates and not feel ashamed; to feel that he is accepted and honored by the group whose opinions he values. This want is so strong and so broad in its influence that it is undoubtedly the primary motivating cause of more things that each one of us does than is any other single want, probably more even than are all of the other wants put together.

In fact, I believe if each one of us were to make a careful analysis of all of the things he does in any one day (other than the routine requirements of his job) he would find that considerably more than three-fourths of all of these things are done directly or indirectly with the desire to increase his feeling of im portance, of personal worthwhileness.

That sounds bad, doesn't it? But actually it is a highly desirable condition.

It is a good thing that you and I do want to feel more important, and it is good too that we spend so much of our time and energy trying to satisfy that want.

It is *what* satisfies the want for a feeling of importance and *how* we go about seeking to satisfy it that make the actions this want causes either good or bad.

In addition to acting as a strong primary cause of action itself, the want for a feeling of importance or worthwhileness also exercises a powerful influence on just what suggestions concerning the other wants will be given any consideration at all by the person; and often it seems to exercise rather poor judgment in which suggestions it accepts and which it rejects.

The explanation is simple. We enjoy so much any experience in which the net total of all we think good or worthwhile about ourselves increases (expansion of the ego) that we tend to prolong that experience. On the other hand, we dislike so strongly any experience in which the net total of this feeling of worthwhileness decreases (deflation of the ego) that we try to bring the experience to an end just as promptly as we can. If we must remain in the company of the person or continue to read the letter or listen to the speech that caused the deflation, we build up an emotional wall, usually anger, which effectively keeps out any further suggestions from that source. And this applies to suggestions which are related entirely to other wants and would probably be accepted and acted upon were it not for the emotional wall or "insulation" with which we have surrounded ourselves.

Did you ever try to reason with a child after you had made him angry? No matter how reasonable your suggestions were, no matter how pleasing to the child they would normally have been, the answer was "No!" It was as if every door to the child's reasonableness had been closed tight and your normally pleasing suggestions were not even heard.

Psychologically, this is exactly what did happen.

And there is not a great deal of difference between the child and the adult, except that the adult has usually (but not always) learned to conceal his emotions more effectively than the child has.

Perhaps I can best illustrate this by an experience of my own which occurred over 30 years ago.

I was personnel director of a large department store. We had an excellent training program, but we felt the need for a good text on the subject of Merchandise Control Methods.

When one of the best known correspondence schools advertised a new course in that subject, I wrote immediately to see if we could purchase several sets of their books. The answer was that the sales representative would be in our city soon and would call on us.

When he came a week or two later, he was shown into my office immediately. Did any salesman ever have a more perfect situation? But here was his opening statement:

"Am I glad to be back in God's country again. I have been down in Florida for the past two weeks and those damn Crackers down there are either too dumb or too lazy to be interested in anything that will improve themselves."

Now it just so happens that I am a Florida Cracker! I was born about a hundred miles south of Jacksonville.

I looked at the books and they were just what we wanted, but, in spite of this, I said that I didn't believe I could make an immediate decision. I really had been authorized to make the purchase and, had the salesman's approach been different, would probably have signed up immediately. But as it was, I waited until the salesman had left the city and then I mailed the order directly to the company.

He probably got full commission for the sale, but at least my pride had been protected by not having to give the order to a man who had insulted my fellow Florida Crackers.

"How silly," you say. *And you are right.*

But I am inclined to believe that two out of three people would have done the same thing, some possibly even worse.

It is of major importance, then, that every contact we may have with any person we would influence should, if possible, begin with something which pleases that person by making him feel a little more important, or, at least, something that does not antagonize him by making him feel less important.

This is true whether the contact be through printed advertising, letter, public speech, or personal conversation.

To live safely, securely, and comfortably. All normal people want to continue to live, and if anyone can be convinced that a given action will make it more certain that he will live, there is a strong probability that he will do that thing. Effective use of this want may be made in safety campaigns, in the sale of certain types of automobile equipment, or in guiding the choice of which of several means of transportation will be used.

For most of us, however, the fear that sudden death may be lurking around every corner does not exist, and efforts to influence us by appealing to the sheer desire to avoid death or dismemberment are not so effective as it would seem they should be.

But there is another want, closely related to the instinct for self-preservation, which some observers have put as the most dominant in the minds of the great mass of working people. It is the *want for a feeling of assurance that their jobs will be reasonably permanent.* There may have been times when this was not true, but in all except boom times this want for a feeling of security is one of the strongest wants of almost everyone. It is not necessary, nor is it even advisable in most cases, to mention the want directly. The more subtle the appeal, the stronger it is; this is true of the appeal to any want.

Also related to the drive for self-preservation is the desire for personal comfort. First immediate safety, then long-range security, then comfort. The advertisement which causes a man to picture himself leaning back comfortably in a chair, custom made and upholstered to fit his exact size and figure, may not be appealing to the most powerful want; but it is a strong one, especially in prosperous times. And having *comfortable* working conditions is often fully as important in promoting morale as having *safe* working conditions, probably because the former are so often neglected.

During World War II there was a demonstration of how a desire for continued comfort may have even more effect on our actions than fear of sudden death. For years every effort had been made to reduce the number of accidents by telling people of the dangers of fast driving. Then came the announcement that when our present tires were gone it would be practically impossible to get new ones. Immediately we all began to drive more slowly, more carefully, and traffic accidents were reduced. We would not slow down to save our lives, but when it looked as if we must slow down or give up our automobiles and ride the streetcars and buses, we slowed down.

To find the right mate and rear a family. This, also, is a strong want. It may, at times, be even stronger in its influence than the desire to live. Most safety workers have found this to be a fact. A picture of a mother and children waiting at home for the father, who, because he has been careless, will never come home, has a stronger appeal even than the appeal to the man's own desire to live. Where the person has a family, the skillful leader mentions it as often as possible. He asks about a child who has been sick or comments about a son or daughter who has won a prize in school, indicating that he remembers both that the person has a family and some of the details about the family.

To explore the unknown. We are all explorers at heart, and that has been true since infancy. Curiosity is one of the earliest of the instincts that influence the behavior of an infant, and its influence continues through life. While most of us do not have nearly so great an opportunity to use this want to influence people as does the advertiser, we can occasionally do so.

Occasionally to forget the cares and problems of life and to play or to be entertained, to escape the humdrum. For the great majority of people, their work itself, if taken in a matter-of-fact, practical, realistic way, is somewhat humdrum. But everyone likes, at times, to escape the humdrum and have a little excitement. Many must satisfy this hunger by going to the movies, the ball game, or in some similar way, rather than in their work. But the more the work can be given some of the elements of a game, if this is not carried too far, the better it is. Almost everyone likes to enter competition, to play a game. That is why so many men like to speak of their work as a "game." All competitions for prizes and charts showing the relative standing of different departments, whether in a business organization, a Sunday school, or a club, appeal to this love of competition. Frequently the desire to win and to be recognized as a winner is even greater than the desire for the actual cash reward. Contests thus often appeal to the want for a feeling of importance as well as to the fun of playing a game.

Step 2. Plan the appeal to reach as many wants as possible.

For an appeal to be the most effective in producing sustained effort, as many of the five fundamental wants as possible should be brought into play.

The reason why anything offering the possibility of increased earnings has so strong and so broad an appeal is that, no matter what anyone's desires may be, the realization of practically all of them can be brought nearer by the possession of more money, properly used. In an appeal to the want for more money (true of all wants, but especially of this one) we should try to know and to mention the specific reason for the want—son just entering college, desire to pay off the mortgage, etc. This combines a man's want to be remembered with the want to do more for his family.

Step 3. Decide the order in which the wants should be introduced.

Some judgment should be exercised in choosing which want should be mentioned first when two or more wants are being used to influence action.

Here is a case in which two wants were used some weeks before Christmas in an endeavor to get us to mail our packages early. The radio announcement made several times each day was approximately as follows:

Christmas is one day nearer. Mail your packages soon. You will make it easier for the mail carrier and be surer that your own packages will arrive safely and on time.

We all have a warm spot in our hearts for the mail carrier who delivers our mail in good weather and bad. Especially do we sympathize with him at Christmas time. So if we feel that we are doing something to make his task a little easier, it gives us a much-to-be-desired glow of satisfaction which comes from having done a good deed. Then if, incidentally, we do get our packages delivered safely and promptly that is good too.

However, the appeal would have been much less effective had the more selfish part of the motivation been omitted. But, out of fairness to us humans, it should be added, also, that it would have been much less effective if *only* the selfish motivation had been used.

So, if there is an altruistic motive with strong appeal as well as a selfish motive, we should, as a rule, mention the altruistic motive first. It makes a person feel a little more important when we compliment him by indicating that we believe him to be a person influenced by altruistic motives. But we should quickly and tactfully introduce also the more selfish motive.

Step 4. Present your case tactfully, always keeping the wants of the other person in the forefront.

It should always be remembered, as was brought out earlier in the chapter, that the desire for a feeling of importance serves also as a "doorkeeper" for all of the wants and, if offended, can *and frequently will,* prevent reasonable consideration of suggestions, no matter how desirable they may be.

The rule to be followed is also given earlier in this chapter, but it is so important that it bears repeating:

It is of major importance that every contact we may have with any person we would influence should, wherever possible, begin with something which will please that person by making him feel a little more important, or at least, something that will not antagonize him by making him feel less important.

Step 5. Follow-up.

The problems of influencing behavior would be simple indeed if our suggestions and instructions had no competition, but such is not the case.

We would not expect a rosebush to live and prosper in our garden without any further attention, even though it has been planted carefully and correctly. The same is true of an idea.

No matter how skillfully we may have established the relationship between the person's wants and doing what we want him to do, even no matter how many or how strong are the wants to which we have appealed, reasonably frequent and tactful follow-up is necessary.

Like the rosebush, the idea we have planted must be nurtured or it will often die.

We must find opportunities, from time to time, to keep the idea fresh in the person's mind. But we must be careful not to overdo this and give the feeling that we are nagging.

A Problem in Influencing Behavior

This is an actual case which happened in a large department store several years ago. Names and some other details are changed.

Assume that you are Mr. Smith, Superintendent of Selling. You are 35 years old and have been in the organization about three years.

Mr. Young is the best salesman in the hardware department. He is about 60 years old and has been in the hardware department over 30 years. You are very much interested in building various things around the house, and Mr. Young has frequently helped you with your carpentering problems, so you and he have become good friends.

Recently a much improved system for OK'ing charges has been installed, and the general manager has issued strict orders that all charges must be OK'd before the merchandise is given to the customers.

Mr. Young refuses to have his charges OK'd in advance. He is pleasant about it. He just tells the section manager that it is not necessary since he knows all of his customers and will never lose anything for the house. And so far this has been true.

But the other salesmen, seeing Mr. Young hand out the merchandise, do the same thing and there have been losses.

The section manager has asked you to talk to Mr. Young.

How will you handle it? To what want or wants will you appeal? How will you present the matter tactfully?

How it was actually handled. Mr. Smith sent for Mr. Young.

"Come in Mr. Young, have a seat. I have a problem in your department which I would like very much to have you help me with, if you will."

"What is it, Mr. Smith?"

"We are having trouble getting most of the men in your department to have their charges OK'd. They all look up to you as their model, and anything they see you do they think is all right for them to do. We have not lost any money yet on your charges, but we have lost quite a little on theirs. I believe, Mr. Young, if you will follow the rule and have your charges OK'd, they will immediately do the same."

"I see your problem, Mr. Smith, and I surely would like to help, but I hate to embarrass customers I have been waiting on for years by having them see me getting their charge accounts OK'd, something I have never had to do before."

"I have an idea which will help that, Mr. Young. We can move the charge phone back behind the scenes to the location where you wrap the packages. It takes only a few seconds to OK most purchases, and your customers would not see you at all."

"Thank you Mr. Smith. Since you explained the matter the way you did, I have decided to have my purchases OK'd anyway, but I hope you can have the phone moved. It surely is embarrassing as it is now."

"I was sure you would help when you understood our problem, Mr. Young. I will have the phone moved as soon as I can.

"There is one thing more I want to ask you while you are here. Mrs. Smith has been getting after me to put some Early American hinges and catches on the kitchen cabinets. Do you have anything like that?"

"We surely do, Mr. Smith, and in several sizes. I'll be glad to show them to you any time."

Comment

Mr. Young's refusal to have his charges OK'd in advance was probably caused as much by his desire to protect his own feeling of importance (not wanting to let the customer know that he was no longer permitted to OK the charges himself) as it was to his desire to save his customers embarrassment. But, of course, Mr. Smith did not mention this. It would not have been tactful.

His approach was for him, the executive, to give to Mr. Young, the salesman, an increased sense of importance by *asking his help* and mentioning how the other salesmen looked up to him (which they did).

Also, moving the charge phone showed that Mr. Smith understood Mr. Young's feelings and wanted to make the request for compliance as reasonable as possible.

The closing remarks about the Early American fittings put the relationship back on the old friendly basis and largely wiped out any feeling that this was just a "corrective interview."

Incidentally, wherever necessary and practicable, charge phones throughout the store were moved to less conspicuous locations.

6

HOW TO MAKE AND KEEP FRIENDS

The deepest principle of human nature is the craving to be appreciated.
—WILLIAM JAMES.

NO ONE CAN ACHIEVE TRULY SATISFYING SUCCESS alone. We all need the help of others. We need the feeling that we are accepted by some group. We need to be liked.

For some the accomplishment of these important steps toward real success comes naturally. They seem instinctively to know what to do and say to cause people to like them and to enjoy doing things with and for them.

But for most of us there is a need, first to learn just what behavior on our part will cause people to like us and to enjoy doing things with us and for us, and then consciously and consistently to endeavor to make that behavior a natural part of our everyday living.

Fortunately, the things we must do are those simple acts of courtesy which are within the power of anyone if he has a sincere desire to please people and will give a reasonable amount of attention to the task of doing so. Here are a few suggestions:

Greet People Pleasantly and Promptly

There are few experiences more unpleasant than to enter a room where several people are gathered informally and not to be noticed or spoken to by anyone. And how grateful we always are to the person who gives us a nod of recognition and a welcoming smile and possibly moves over a little to make room for us. Little things like that play a much larger role in making friends than we may think. And the reason why they do is simple. Not to be noticed at all is one of the most ego-deflating experiences anyone can have. Therefore, the person who saves us from that unpleasant experience has done us a really substantial service. He is the kind of person we like and want as a friend.

Remember Names and Use Them Frequently

There is probably no one thing which pleases any person more than to be greeted *by name*. This is especially true when the person is a new member of the group or, for any other reason, hardly expects his name to be remembered.

If you find it difficult to remember names and faces, here is a simple and practical program which, followed carefully and persistently, will, in large measure, eliminate that difficulty:

1. *Get the name CLEARLY when it is first mentioned.* Too often a name is spoken rapidly and somewhat indistinctly in the introduction and we go ahead with the conversation thinking that we shall get it later. It never offends anyone if you say, "I always like to get a person's name correctly; do you mind repeating your name?" If the name is one which may be spelled in either of two ways, as "Green" or "Greene," spell it back, "G-R-E-E-N, or do you put an E on the end?" If you are at your desk, you can be casually writing the name down on a piece of paper as you spell it. If, later in the conversation, the name slips out of your memory,

you can glance at the paper. Also, for many persons, writing a name and seeing it in writing impresses it on the memory more strongly than would repeating it several times.

If time permits, some such comment as, "I have a good friend who came from down near Atlanta, named Sam Greene; are you, by any chance, related to him?" This ties the name to a known name, and you can also be making mental comparisons between the two men in size, weight, and appearance.

All of this seems like a rather long-drawn-out program which will take much more time than can be spared, but it usually takes only one or two minutes at most—no more than the useless exchange of remarks about the weather so often used as a "warm-up" conversation—and it is much more profitable to you and pleasing to the person with whom you are talking.

2. *Repeat the name frequently during the conversation, especially during the first conversation.* Most people who have unusually good memories for names will repeat the name of the person they are talking with as many as eight to ten times even in a short conversation: "Yes, Miss Jones, I think you are right," and "Miss Jones, have you heard," etc. All of this takes practically no time and is distinctly pleasing to the persons with whom they talk. This should, of course, not be overdone.

3. *Form an association between the name and some characteristic of the person.* Try, thus, to find some way to tie the name to the person. For example, Mr. Joiner wears a Masonic emblem, so he must have "joined" the Masonic lodge. Mr. Schnell talks very slowly, just the opposite of his name. "Schnell" is the German word for quick.

Sometimes the connection is between name and personal appearance and, if so, that is excellent. Mr. Hardy is tall, powerfully built, deeply tanned—anything but frail. So the word "hardy" just seems to fit. Mr. Green is tall, and I remember an old saying, "When you are green you are growing." With a little practice, some such connection between the name and what one does or what one looks like can be established for almost everyone. Even when it cannot, the study of the person and his name, made in an effort, even an unsuccessful effort, to establish a connection, helps to fix the name and characteristics.

4. *Use a systematic method of describing personal appearance.* It is surprising how little we remember, even about things we see every day, unless we consciously and systematically observe them. No better illustration of this can be found than to ask the average man to make a sketch of his watch dial. Try it yourself. Unless you are more keenly observant than nine out of ten persons, you will forget many things.

One executive who visited the many plants of a large corporation on the average of only once a year developed a code for his notebook by which he entered a brief description of each of the 30 or 40 key persons in each plant.

This developed the habit of systematic observation and, also, furnished a permanent record which he reviewed just before visiting each plant.

It is strongly recommended to anyone who has difficulty in remembering names and faces that, for a time at least, he adopt the practice of writing down, at the first opportunity, brief descriptions of those whom he meets.

When this practice is first started, he will probably be surprised at the meagerness of the information remembered, but observation soon becomes systematic and almost unconscious, and a more adequate description can be written.

5. *Proceed thoughtfully, conscientiously, persistently.* Success may not come overnight. Associations, carefully thought out, will become all confused. Attempts to "observe" so as to be able to write an accurate description will take the mind off the subject of the conversation. All of these things are discouraging, but time and time again this technique, when applied thoughtfully, con-

scientiously, and persistently, has overcome these difficulties, and has built real skill in remembering names and faces. Stick to it.

Listen More Than You Talk

The surest way to win the reputation of being a most interesting conversationalist, one who is always welcome anywhere, is to form the habit of finding out what the other person's interests are and then asking just enough questions to get him to talking about those interests. Strangely enough, even when a man has a proposition to "sell" or an argument to win, he usually is more successful when he allows the other person to do a large part of the talking than he is when he endeavors to dominate the conversation.

More than one applicant has successfully "sold" himself to an executive by listening attentively as that executive tells of his ideas on how a department should be run, and commenting briefly from time to time on how fully he agrees.

Too many of us, however, even when we are supposed to be listening, are thinking more about what *we* plan to say next than about what the other person is saying. That is not really listening; it is merely waiting somewhat impatiently for a chance to cut in again with our comments. And that type of listening does not make friends.

We should be interested in what the other person says and show it!

Show Your Appreciation

The desire for appreciation is one of the strongest wants in all of us. In fact, many psychologists believe it to be the dominating influence in our lives.

So it is natural that we should like the people who let us know that they appreciate the things, even the little things, we do for them.

And this regular expression of appreciation for little things done and for the love that prompted the doing is one of the most important requirements for a happy family life.

Expressions of appreciation need not be formal to please people. In fact, it may be that little informal words of appreciation included in everyday conversation are even more effective in friend-making than are the more formal statements, because they can be used so much more frequently and seem less artificial.

There was an example of this in a telephone conversation I overheard a few days ago. One of the members of a committee had been unable to attend a meeting and had asked Mrs. Halsey to tell her what had been decided. Here is what I heard:

"Mrs. King, you asked me to call you about the meeting of the Senior-Citizen Committee. We had a most interesting meeting, but we surely missed you. Mrs. Brown suggested, etc."

I am afraid had someone asked me to report on a meeting I would have omitted the "but we surely missed you"—not intentionally, of course, just thoughtlessly.

The habit of giving credit regularly in conversation for things other people have done for us or shown us is another one of the little things that make people like us. For example, someone comments favorably on something you are doing, and you might say something like, "Bill Jenkins showed me that trick and it surely does save time."

And it is especially important to give credit to the employee who made the suggestion when your chief comments favorably on something in your department. It builds morale in the department and makes your chief think more highly of you.

Little things, little things, all little things. But just such little things make the difference between tact and lack of tact, between causing your associates and your employees to like you or having them merely tolerate you, between success or failure on any job which involves meeting and influencing people—and how few jobs there are which do not require this.

Say "Will You" Rather Than "You Must."

Did you ever call on someone, possibly at his request and to do him a favor, and have some clerk tell you, "You'll have to wait, Mr. Brown is busy just now"? Didn't you feel like saying, "I don't 'have to' do anything of the kind; I'll just walk out"?

Such expressions as "you have to" or "you must" should seldom if ever be used, even when you have the authority to do this. Even if "will you" fails to get the desired result—as when, for example, an applicant continues to object to giving some information you are required to get from him to complete a form—some such statement as "I am sorry, but I am required to get that information before I can send in your application" is much less antagonizing than "You have to give us that information." There is a subtle distinction between "*I* am required" and "*You* are required," which makes the former much less antagonizing than the latter even though both you and I know that they mean exactly the same thing. I am the one who is taking the stigma of admitting that I must obey rules and orders instead of making you the one. And this simple, almost silly, little distinction means much more in pleasing people than it seems reasonable to believe it could mean.

Try to Have a Reasonably Wide Circle of Friends

It is highly desirable for any person who aspires to a successful career in buisness to have a reasonably wide circle of friends, and they should be people of many occupations and interests.

He should be interested in and take an active part in such organizations as chambers of commerce, trade associations, and luncheon clubs, but he should never be so active that he neglects his own business. He will find that being active in his church and Sunday School will be doubly rewarding—for the spiritual values and an opportunity to develop leadership in voluntary groups.

Out of this wide circle of friends the young aspirant to success in business should choose with great care a few close friends. They should be people who inspire him to work hard to achieve success rather than those who, through their own contentment with the mediocre, cause him to set lower and easier goals for himself.

And, above all, they should be people with high standards of business ethics, morality, and general conduct. In these important things, too, they should inspire him to strive constantly to do better.

Remember That Your Employees, Too, Like Appreciation

This is discussed more fully in Chapter 8, but it is so important that it bears repeating here.

This is true because it is probably even more important to your success and happiness that you have the good will and cooperation of those with whom you associate every day on the job than it is to have the friendship of people in general, as important as that is. And it is, indeed, important.

Real cooperation from your employees and associates on the job *cannot be bought with money*—but this will be discussed later. Just two short stories from my own experience now:

I remember, almost as if it were yesterday, something which happened about 40 years ago. I had just been employed as personnel director of a large department store, my first job as a personnel director. The employment manager (also new on the job) and I thought up a plan which we believed would greatly simplify the work of our office. The employment manager was an excellent draftsman and he drew up the suggestion in fine form.

We sent it to the vice-president who had charge of our work. After a reasonable time it came back with this note:

"Excellent suggestion both in the plan suggested and the form in which it is submitted. Put it into effect."

That, as I said, was about 40 years ago, but I am still an enthusiastic booster for that store.

Some years later in another organization, I made a suggestion and here was the answer:

"I just asked for the facts from the personnel records. When I want your suggestions I'll ask for them."

I was with that organization only a short time and was most happy when someone offered me another job even though it was at a lower salary.

One Simple Rule for Making and Keeping Friends

Perhaps all of this can be summarized in one simple rule which should be applied every day in our contacts with people. It is:

RULE FOR MAKING AND KEEPING FRIENDS

> Always take every honest opportunity to say and do those things which make people feel bigger, better, more important.
>
> Never, unless it is absolutely necessary for their own good or unless circumstances allow no alternative, say or do those things, *even in a joke,* which hurt people's feelings, which make them feel smaller, meaner, less important.

And favorable comments should not be limited to things which are immediately apparent, such as an attractive hat or dress, an interesting talk just completed, or a piece of work done unusually well. When we read in the paper or hear of some such event as a son or daughter of a friend winning honors, we should always remember to congratulate at the earliest opportunity both the young people themselves and the father and mother. Even if the news item is just that the child has gone to some camp for the summer, we should mention it and express the hope that the child will have a fine time. It is well to use the child's name if it is remembered. This adds to the "ego-expanding" power of the comment more than would seem possible.

Any comment which shows that we have remembered something about the person to whom we are talking always has more ego-expanding power (and, therefore, is more pleasing) than an equally pleasant or complimentary remark about something we can see at the moment.

It is almost unbelievable how important just being remembered is to the happiness of everyone.

All of this probably sounds as if it would be quite easy to do, but it is not.

There is something in the make-up of each one of us which causes the carrying out of these suggestions to be more difficult than it seems reasonable to believe that it would be.

Perhaps this can be illustrated best by a personal experience which occurred a few years ago.

The One Personal Quality Most Important to Success in Pleasing and Influencing People

I had agreed to speak on this subject to a group of young business executives. As I was anxious to give this group something worthwhile, I read two or three of the best books I could find on the development of personality and prepared my talk most carefully. It was a rather elaborate speech, and I was proud of it as a literary effort, but I had the feeling that it did not really give any definite and concrete answer to the question these young people were expecting me to answer for them.

Fortunately, the speech was never used. Something happened on the morning of the day on which I was to give the talk that made me throw away all I had prepared, because it gave to me what is, I believe, the real answer to my question. And that answer, like almost all important truths, does not have any big words in it. Let me tell the story.

That morning I came into the office a few moments late and as I approached my secretary's desk she said:

"I have a surprise for you this morning, Mr. Halsey, your royalty check is here."

She knew that there was a large insurance premium to be paid that month and was enthusiastic about the whole thing, being most happy to be the bearer of good news.

"Isn't that fine. It surely came at exactly the right time, didn't it?"

That is what I should have said. But there is one part of the story which my secretary did not know. Royalty checks come on time each six months so regularly that the arrival of this check, though of course quite welcome, was certainly no surprise. Also, I knew the exact amount due. *So my answer was just exactly what it should not have been:*

"Oh, that," I said, "I knew it was coming. I thought at first that you had a real surprise."

"Oh," she replied, and I know she must have felt the way a toy balloon looks when you let the air out of it.

I went on into my office thinking about the incident and worrying about it. It was one of those things one does worry about because he knows that it would be made worse by apologizing. Suddenly the idea came to me that here was the answer to my problem. The quality most necessary for success in pleasing and influencing people is not something with a high-sounding psychological name. It is just this:

The willingness and ability one has to understand and to control in himself, the strong natural tendency always present in everyone to say and do those things which will protect or enhance his own ego.

You might say that this does not apply at all to the incident I have just related. Surely I did not say that I knew about the royalty check with any conscious desire to "show off."

Of course, I did not! But it is a fundamental fact of human nature that the one thing which each person wants more than he wants anything else is a feeling of increasing personal importance—an expansion of the ego. This want, or *hunger* as we should probably call it, is so strong and so continuously present that we are constantly doing things—often unconsciously—which will in some measure satisfy it. It would not seem, however, that such a silly little thing as knowing some trifling fact which someone else does not know would satisfy this hunger at all—but it does. So it was a desire to satisfy this fundamental hunger for a feeling of importance—a desire not consciously felt or identified by me at the moment, it is true, but there nevertheless—which caused me to blurt out the remark I did.

And it is the replacing of just such thoughtless remarks with remarks that thoughtfully take into account the fact that the other person, too, has a desire for a feeling of increasing importance which is the largest single factor in pleasing and influencing people.

Let me illustrate how easy it is *not* to do this. If someone tells a joke we have previously read, we will probably first make some such remark as:

"That's a good one isn't it—so true to life."

But after we have made this polite and pleasing comment, all too often we cannot resist the temptation of showing that we, too, have read the magazine and so we spoil it all by adding:

"It was in last Sunday's *Times* wasn't it?"

And we all know at least one person who spoils every story we tell by always having caught a fish just two pounds heavier than the one we have been bragging just a little about, or by telling about a man *ninety-seven* years old who milked *eight* cows every day when we have just finished telling, with considerable pride, about an uncle who, at the ripe old age of *ninety-six,* milked *seven* cows every day.

Instinctively, we all dislike and avoid those persons who "make us feel cheap" by doing these annoying little things *even though we know that they do them quite unconsciously and with no thought of offending.*

The consequences of this all-too-common tendency to forget that the other fellow, too, has an ego has as harmful an effect on business success as it does on social popularity.

For example, there was the case of Fred Simpson, an otherwise capable executive who sincerely wanted the suggestions and help of everyone.

He had recently come into the organization as general manager, promoted from one of the smaller plants owned by the same corporation.

He decided quite wisely that in this larger organization he would need the cooperation of all the other executives and junior executives if he was to succeed. So he called them together for a meeting at which he assured them quite sincerely that he wanted and would welcome their suggestions on any phase of the business.

One problem was especially troublesome and he asked Charlie Livingston, one of the most alert younger executives, if he and three of his assistants would study the situation together and let him have their suggestions.

They went to work on the problem with great enthusiasm and in a reasonable time had a carefully prepared report ready for presentation.

Charlie made an appointment for the committee to meet with Mr. Simpson and quite enthusiastically presented the committee's suggestions. Here was Mr. Simpson's answer:

"That's fine, Charlie. You boys are right on the beam."

Excellent; or rather it would have been if he had stopped there, *but he did not.* He went on to say:

"Just to show how clearly you boys are thinking, I want to tell you that Mr. Brown (the assistant general manager) and I discussed this question yesterday and I decided to do exactly what you have recommended. Your committee is doing good work, Charlie, keep it up."

That is all he said, *but he might as well have said:*

"You boys are *good,* Charlie; but, of course, not *quite* as good as I am."

How do you think Charlie and the other members of the committee felt as they walked out of the chief's office, and how enthusiastically would they work on new suggestions?

You know the answer. The employee participation plan in that organization was all but dead just because of one thoughtless remark.

This was true because in business, as in social life, we all dislike and avoid those persons who make us feel small and unimportant by saying such ego-robbing things, and we do not, if we can help it, expose ourselves again to situations in which we are likely to repeat unpleasant experiences.

I wonder, in *our own* everyday contacts with people generally and especially with the people under our supervision, if we are not all guilty at times of saying and doing things (unintentionally, of course) which take away some of their enthusiasm. I know I am, and I was surprised when I began to watch for this in my own behavior to see how often it did appear.

No one of us would be guilty, of course, if he could only think of the effect of what he is going to say before he says it.

But how can anyone succeed in doing that?

It has helped me in my own efforts to avoid doing these things to think of each situation where two or more people meet as offering just so much "ego food," just as if there were a table in the middle of the group with a box of candy on it. If any person grabs more than his share, someone must go without—and no one likes to do that.

Often, now, just as I am on the verge of blurting out some thoughtless remark, the picture of that table comes to my mind and I decide that I do not want to be an "ego-food hog." This simple little device has helped me so much that I feel sure it will help anyone who will try it.

Also, there is one important way in which "ego food" differs from ordinary food. If I restrain my desire for the larger piece of candy and take the smaller one, I do definitely have less food, and my hunger for candy is not so fully satisfied. But, if I restrain my natural tendency to show off a little and do not tell the "one better" which I know after someone else has told a story, there comes to me a feeling of satisfaction because I have exercised self-control and done an unselfish thing. And if I continue to do this, I experience the even greater satisfaction of having people like me, of seeing faces light up and the circle open when I join any group where I am known.

All this is "ego food"—much finer than I would have got had I grabbed more than my share in the first instance. It is as if I were being rewarded for restraining my natural tendency to grab the one large piece of cheap candy by being given a whole box of fine candy.

SELF RATING OF YOUR "FRIEND-MAKING" QUALITIES AND PRACTICES

Following the instructions and using the rating scale given at the close of Chapter 3, answer each question by writing in the space provided the letter (or letters) which will indicate your carefully considered opinion of the extent to which you do the things described in the question.

1. To what extent do you take advantage of every opportunity to go to places where you will meet new people, such as conventions, club meetings, community forums, Sunday School, and church? ______

2. When you do go, to what extent do you make it a point to get acquainted with as many people as possible rather than to stay continuously with your own small group? ______

3. To what extent do you make an effort to get each person's name clearly when you are introduced, always asking tactfully what the name is when you do not get it at first? ______

4. To what extent do you use frequently in conversation the name of the person to whom you are speaking, both new and old acquaintances? ______

5. How skillful are you in getting people, especially new acquaintances, to talk about themselves, their experiences, their families, and how regularly do you do this? ______

6. How regularly do you remember to tell people about things you have read or heard that you know will please them, such as having seen in the paper about a son or daughter who has won honors or having heard someone make a complimentary remark about the person? ______

7. To what extent do you regularly observe and make pleasing comments about such things as a becoming hat or dress, an attractive home or garden, or a piece of work done unusually well in office or shop? ______

8. How fully do you refrain from saying or doing, even in a joke, anything which will make the other person feel smaller, meaner, or less important? ______

9. How completely do you keep free from periods of moodiness or absent-mindedness which cause you to neglect the little courtesies which please people? ______

10. How successful are you in so controlling emotional reactions that you seldom, if ever, blurt out thoughtless remarks that hurt people's feelings, remarks that, if you had thought a moment, you would not have made? ______

11. To what extent do you make it a point to admit to the persons concerned that you have made a mistake when later developments show that you have been wrong in some opinion you have asserted quite strongly? ______

12. To what extent do you refrain from following each story someone else tells of something he or a relative has done by telling a story yourself of how you or someone you know has done even better? (Think carefully before you answer this one. It is a most common failing.) ______

13. To what extent do you do things to please and help your friends at the cost of some personal inconvenience—go to see them when sick, write to them even when you are very busy, offer your services promptly and neglect your own pleasure to help at the time of a death or serious illness? ______

14. When you have found it necessary to refuse requests, to what extent have you been able to do this in so tactful a manner that the person refused was not offended? ______

15. How fully do you refrain from needless saying of unkind things about people who are not present, even when those things are definitely known by you to be true? ______

16. To what extent do your friends come to you to tell you of their difficulties and ask for advice and help? ______

17. Who is the most likable person you know, the person everyone always seems to be most happy to see? Decide carefully and then write, in the space provided below, two or three of the characteristics of his (or her) personality which you believe make him (or her) so likable.

1. ______________________
2. ______________________
3. ______________________

Now, rate yourself on how fully you believe these same things to be present in your personality. ______

18. Think now of some person you do not like too well, not because of anything wrong with his (or her) character, but because you just don't like him (or her). Decide what one or two characteristics of his (or her) personality cause you to feel as you do.

1. ______________________
2. ______________________

Now, rate yourself on how fully you believe your personality to be free from these things. ______

19. How thoughtfully and wisely have you made an effort to associate with and choose your friends from groups in which the ideals and character of the members are such that doing the things you must do to gain recognition will not eventually bring unhappiness to your family or to you? ______

After considering carefully your answers to all of these 19 questions, but not necessarily trying to strike an average, how do you rate yourself on "friend-making" qualities and practices? [ ]

No matter how good your total score is, you would, of course, like to be better. Study the questions you marked the lowest and plan to work on these *one at a time*. Give especial attention the first week to one. The next week work on another (without dropping the gains made on the first), and so on to the end. Then start all over again.

This is an interesting game, but more than that it is probably the most profitable investment of your time you can possibly make. It is an investment which, if made thoughtfully, conscientiously, persistently, will pay big dividends in success and happiness.

7

HOW TO GET REAL COOPERATION FROM THOSE YOU SUPERVISE[1]

NO ONE CAN HOPE TO ACHIEVE ANY LARGE MEASURE of success without the help of others—especially without the capable, intelligent, and enthusiastic cooperation of the members of the team which he supervises.

Much research has been carried out over a long period of years in an effort to find out what one must do to deserve and get such cooperation, and some interesting discoveries have been made. Probably the most startling of these is that, whether or not the worker finds in his work a source of personal satisfaction and pride, whether or not he likes and trusts his supervisor, and whether or not his everyday contacts with his fellow workers are pleasant, all have a much greater effect on his output, even in a routine job, than it ever had before been believed could be possible.

This is true because all of these things together create that something called *morale* which, although purely emotional itself,

[1] This chapter is largely summarized, with permission of the publisher, from the fuller discussion in the author's book, *Supervising People* (New York: Harper & Brothers, 2nd edition, 1953).

so controls and conditions physical and mental responses that it enables the worker to turn out more and better work without any increase in fatigue and causes him to enter enthusiastically into the activities and endeavors of the group with which he works.

Out of a careful study of all of the findings of this research and from my own experience of more than 40 years in this field have come the nine rules which follow, no one of which we may safely disregard and hope to get the full cooperation of those we supervise.

1. Make a constant and intelligent effort to be absolutely fair in your every relationship with those you supervise.

I have discussed the principles and techniques of supervising people with many groups of executives and first-line supervisors in different parts of the country. In almost every case I have asked the group to vote on the question, "What do you consider to be the most important requirement for success in supervising people?"

Almost without exception the vote was for *fairness.*

The keynote of the whole policy of personnel management, whether it be of a small group or a working force of many thousands, should be a constant endeavor to achieve *fairness.*

But the achievement of fairness requires much more than an admonition on the part of top management that there shall be fairness, more even than the sincere wish and intention of everyone to be fair. Sound management must provide systems and records so that the supervisors and others who must make decisions will have all of the facts before them. And it must provide training in the use of these systems and records so that the wish to be fair can be translated into actual fairness.

But even being fair is not enough in building real cooperation. The enthusiastic desire to cooperate is based on how the worker *feels* about things. And this feeling, all too often, is at variance with the actual facts.

For example, in choosing between two men for promotion, being careful to be absolutely fair is most important, but it is not enough. The man *not* chosen must have it explained to him the reasons why he was not chosen, and he must, if possible, be convinced that these reasons are sound and fair.

And, when talking to applicants or new employees, executives should be most careful not to make statements which can be misconstrued as being promises. I have often had new employees come to my office after a short period of employment and say that the supervisor had "definitely promised" a salary increase at that time, when all he had said was that it was possible if the person showed unusual ability that he might be given an increase then. When talking to applicants or new employees it should always be remembered that a perfectly general statement such as this will often be taken as a promise and hard feelings will be caused.

2. *Exercise care and skill in selecting the person who is to be assigned to each task.*

For any person to find in his work a source of satisfying self expression he must be able to do that work well.

There is little chance of his being happy in his work if he does not possess the intellect, aptitude, and temperament required to do the work successfully. Nor will he be happy if the work is so simple that it uses only a fraction of the intellect or skill he possesses.

There must be a reasonably close matching of all of the characteristics of the person with the requirements of the job. Without this there can be little hope of the full and enthusiastic cooperation we desire.

A few suggestions follow:

The first of these is so obvious that it seems almost unnecessary to mention it. Yet it is so frequently not followed, but so important, that if I were allowed only one suggestion I believe this would be that one.

It is simply this: *Know the requirements of the job, and keep these requirements constantly in mind during the entire selection process.*

All of us—and I definitely include myself—much too often undertake the task of selecting people without first giving careful thought to *exactly what the person will be required to do* and, even more frequently, *what qualities, physical, mental, and emotional,* are required for fully satisfactory performance.

And unless this is done most carefully serious mistakes will often be made. Let me illustrate with a personal experience:

I had just been appointed to my first industrial personnel job, as employment manager of the Cincinnati Milling Machine Company. My first requisition was for a painter in the casting painting department. I was in luck. Just a day or two before I had interviewed and taken the application of a man with exactly the experience wanted. And his last employer had given him an excellent reference.

Rather good service from the new employment manager, wasn't it? In fact, I was quite proud of myself.

About two days later the foreman came storming into my office. The man could not do the work at all.

One of the requirements of the job was the ability to move the rather heavy castings which were being painted. The man had a serious hernia and could do no heavy lifting.

I had neglected to find out about this most important job requirement.

And it is by no means only inexperienced employment managers who make such mistakes.

In fact, it is my carefully considered opinion that at least half of all of the mistakes made in the selection of employees are due either to not knowing or to overlooking the requirements for success on the job.

The only way I know of to avoid such errors is to prepare some form of selection plan in writing.

Larger organizations usually have complete job specifications for each position. But for the executive selecting someone to work in his own department, a simple mimeographed form, with the requested information filled in in pencil by the executive himself, will probably be even more helpful.

This should be a one-page form with the following headings and space after each for the necessary information.

1. Principal duties of the position.
2. Unusual, disagreeable, or especially demanding duties.
3. Physical requirements and how measured.
4. Skill requirements and how measured.
5. Mental requirements and how measured.
6. Emotional requirements and how measured.
7. Any added comment.

As shown on the form, in addition to a listing of the qualities required, the executive is asked to indicate what method will be used to measure the degree to which the applicant possesses each quality. Some can best be determined from the application blank, others by tests, and others by the interview.

For example, you are to select a new secretary and no one is available for promotion. Experience, skill in shorthand and typing have been determined from the application, by checking the references, and by the use of tests.

But in addition to this you have decided that tact is an important qualification, and that you will determine whether the applicant possesses this quality during the interview.

Obviously, asking the question, "Are you tactful?" would not bring out much valid evidence.

But the following question probably would: "As you know, one of the most important duties of a secretary to an executive is to get other executives in the business to do certain things the way she knows her chief wants them done, and she must often do this without asking her chief to issue orders. Have you ever had any cases where the other executives were a little slow about doing things or sent in some report which you knew would not give your chief the information he wanted?"

Almost every secretary who has had the type of experience you want will answer that she has had just such problems to solve. The next question would, naturally, be, "Just how did you go about correcting that condition?"

This is an example of the application of one of the most important and probably the most frequently ignored rule for good interviewing. It is:

Ask questions which call for narrative statements—things done which have demonstrated the possession of certain qualities—rather than questions calling for an expression of opinions or a mere chronological statement of experience.

3. *Make sure that the introduction to the job of new or transferred employees is friendly, skillful, and adequate.*

The first few days for almost anyone on a new job are difficult and trying, especially if he is taking up a new type of work. Any word of welcome and encouragement the supervisor may be able to give the new worker will count much in building that loyalty to the organization so necessary to the best work. And, conversely, any careless criticism or any indication of dissatisfaction at how inexperienced the new worker is may create a sore spot which will take months to heal.

More can be done to make or mar the new employee's future in the first few days than in weeks at any other time.

Even though you may have assigned the training of the new

employee to an assistant, you should take time yourself to make the new person feel at home. This need not take much time.

Perhaps the most important single moment in the induction process in your department is that in which you, as the new employee's supervisor, receive him from the representative of the employment office who has brought him to you. Here are two examples. In both cases the supervisor was busy with something important and could not, at the moment, do more than say a few words.

In the first case, Bill Hastings was the supervisor. Charlie Williams, the assistant employment manager, brought the new employee into the department shortly after opening time. Bill had talked to him when he was being considered for the job, but seemed to have forgotten this. The assistant employment manager opened the conversation:

"Hello, Bill, I brought you the new man I promised you. Mr. Johnson, this is your new supervisor, Mr. Hastings. I believe you talked with Mr. Johnson before, Bill."

Bill made no comment to indicate that he remembered the interview, but addressed his remarks to Charlie.

"You sure can bring new people at the time when I am most busy, Charlie. He will have to wait awhile until I have time to get him started. Has he ever operated a milling machine?"

"No, Bill, but I am sure he will learn quickly. He had a high score on the tests."

"Maybe, but teaching takes time and I am mighty busy with more important things now. I wish you would bring me someone once in a while who has had some experience. I'll take care of getting him started as soon as I can; I have to get this new job on the machines first."

Charlie showed the new man to a seat near Bill's desk, and left him with the comment: "Don't worry about what Bill said. He is not half so bad as he sounds. He really is a good scout."

In the second case Jim Swain was the supervisor. Immediately after leaving Bill's department, Charlie took Sam Thompson, another new man, to Jim's department. Jim too was busy and could give only a short time at the moment to greeting the new employee, but here is how he handled it. Charlie started in the same way as before:

"Hello, Jim, here is the new man I promised you. Mr. Thompson, this is your new supervisor, Mr. Swain."

"You don't need to introduce me to Mr. Thompson, we had a long talk together a few days ago," and turning to the new employee, "I believe you said your first name is Sam, didn't you? We go by first names around here. Mine is Jim, as I told you. As I remember it, you have never run a turret lathe, but don't let that worry you; from the way Charlie tells me you handled his tests I am counting on you to be one of our best men in a short time. I have got to get this new job started right now, but I will be with you in a little while. Just sit down over by my desk. You can be reading that book about the company they gave you in the employment office. Will you show Sam where the desk is, Charlie?"

Assuming that the two new employees are of equal ability and the jobs of equal difficulty, and that each is turned over to a competent person to be trained, how much longer will it take to transform the first man into a capable and interested worker than it will take to do the same for the second man? An exact answer is impossible, but it will definitely be a considerable period of time —good productive time wasted because the supervisor was so busy getting out production that he didn't have time to be pleasant. And the interesting part of it all is that it probably took as much of Bill's time to explain why he didn't have time to be pleasant as it did for Jim to be pleasant. It usually does.

When *you* are the supervisor and *your* assistant employment manager brings you a new employee at just the moment when everything else seems to need your attention, whose handling of the situation does your greeting of the new employee most closely resemble, that of Bill Hastings or that of Jim Swain?

There are at least three important objectives which we should endeavor to accomplish during the process of introducing an employee to his new assignment. They are: To give him a feeling of confidence in himself, to make sure that he has complete knowledge of the conditions of his employment, and to give him a feeling of pride in his company, his department, and in the work he will be doing.

4. *Find a way to keep each person under your supervision continuously aware that his efforts are appreciated by you.*

Many psychologists believe that the strongest hunger in human nature is a craving to be appreciated; whether or not it actually is the strongest emotional hunger, a feeling that one's efforts are really appreciated is certainly essential to happiness in the work situation and therefore to morale.

Each person in charge of the work of others should take every honest opportunity to say a word of commendation about the work of those under his supervision.

This does not mean that you should spend your entire time making flattering comments to everyone in your department. To do this would probably have an effect quite opposite to that desired, because no one likes empty and insincere flattery. It is disgusting rather than pleasing.

But it does mean that you should consciously and consistently try to look for and comment pleasantly about things that are really worthy of favorable comment. A difficult piece of tabular typing done especially neatly and without error, the completion of a machine operation in better than standard time with a low spoilage record, a sales record that leads the department, are all examples of things that offer such opportunities. Do not fail, also, to comment favorably on any improvement over past performance even though a high standard has not been reached. This is especially true in the case of new employees or those who have recently been corrected because of poor performance.

One caution is probably unnecessary, but consequences of any failure to observe it are so serious that it should be mentioned. It is this: Be most careful to see that too large a share of the complimentary comments is not given to just two or three people in your department even though these people are outstandingly the best and really deserve all you say about them. Do not withhold deserved praise from these people, give them all to which they are entitled, but, also, find some pleasing things to say to the others in your department—all of them.

There is no one whose work is so poor, no one even whose attitude is so poor, that there is not something that can honestly be commended. Take the trouble to find that something and you will probably discover, as so many other executives have, that both quality of work and attitude will improve. There will be more then which can be praised.

An interesting experiment demonstrating the effectiveness of praise in getting school children to do their best work was carried out by Dr. E. B. Hurlock of Teachers College, Columbia University.[2]

A large group of children were first given a test to measure their ability. They were then divided into three groups, carefully selected so that the groups were as nearly equal as possible in ability, in proportion of boys to girls and in average age.

The next day they all assembled in one room for a second test, but before the test was given, the children of Group I were asked to come to the front of the room. They were praised for those

[2] See Journal of Educational Psychology, Vol. XVI, p. 145.

parts of the test in which they had done excellent work on the preceding day, and were encouraged to do even better.

The children of Group II were then called to the front and reproved for the careless mistakes they had made.

The children of Group III heard both praise and reproof, but no comment at all was made to them as to how they had done on the test. They were completely ignored throughout the experiment. A new test was then given and papers collected.

This exact procedure was repeated for four days and the results are shown below:

	First Test	*Second Test*	*Third Test*	*Fourth Test*	*Fifth Test*	*Percent Improvement*
Praised Group	11.81	16.59	18.85	18.81	20.22	71
Reproved Group	11.85	16.59	14.30	13.26	14.19	20
Ignored Group	11.84	14.19	13.30	12.92	12.38	5

While, of course, the results of this one test are by no means conclusive, they do seem to point quite definitely to the fact that encouragement by the use of praise is the most effective method of getting people to do their best work. And this is borne out by the experience of practically every executive I have ever talked with who has taken the trouble to find the things people under his supervision do well and to praise them for these things.

And yet, how frequently many of us are guilty of that poorest of all techniques of supervision—saying nothing. We may assume, as did one high executive I talked with recently, that the people under our supervision should realize that, so long as we do not find any fault with what they are doing, we are satisfied with their work. Or, perhaps, we take the attitude I have heard expressed many times, that people are paid for good work and good work is expected. Why, then, should we praise them when all they are doing is to give what they are paid for?

The answer is simple and practical. We should take the trouble to find the good things people do, to praise them for doing these things, and to offer help and instruction rather than reproof when we cannot praise, because to do this makes people happier in their work than does any other method of supervision. And it has been proved again and again that people who are happy in their work turn out a greater volume of work and work of better quality than do people who are not happy.

But, of course, praise alone of work well done is not enough. There should also be the more tangible evidence of appreciation in the form of increased compensation in proportion to increase in productivity.

Praise will backfire and do more harm than good unless the worker feels that he is fairly paid for what he does and, especially, that no one is paid more, even a little more, unless that person is really worth more.

5. *Give careful and thoughtful consideration to the probable effect each rule, each notice, each practice will have on the feelings of all concerned.*

Closely related to the desire everyone feels "to be appreciated" is the equally strong desire "to be treated like a human being."

Nothing should be required of any worker which will take away any of his pride and self-respect. Arbitrary orders without explanation, criticism in the presence of others, rules or practices which seem to imply suspicion as to one's honesty—to be required to submit to any of these takes away something from a person's self-respect and builds up a resentment against whoever he believes to be responsible.

The resentment is often more bitter and more lasting in its effect than anyone would suspect.

Each one of us in charge of the work of others may be sure that, if we are guilty of such practices, there is resentment, and the more repressed this resentment is the more serious is its effect on morale.

6. Make sure that each person is given adequate training in the duties he is expected to perform.

Once, when I was working with Mr. Samuel W. Reyburn, then president of the Associated Dry Goods Corporation, on a training program for buyers and other executives, he suggested that we put special emphasis on "how to teach," because, in his words:

"I believe that at least half of the work of the average executive is teaching, and the higher he goes in the organization the greater that proportion becomes."

This seemed just a little startling to me at the time, but, since then, I have watched closely the work of many executives and have seen how much of their time actually is spent in what is really teaching. And this teaching is an important part of any executive's work, because through teaching he imparts to others the knowledge and skill he possesses and multiplies his own power to accomplish the desired results. Teaching can also largely eliminate the need for correction and discipline. Most mistakes are caused by lack of knowledge or lack of interest, and both are corrected by really skillful teaching.

Yet few executives have made any specific preparation for this part of their work. The reason is, probably, that most textbooks and articles on the subject deal only in terms of classroom teaching of children.

Here, however, are ten suggestions in summarized form applied directly to the work of the executive in shop, store, or office:

a. *Make the learner want to know.* The good teacher will always "sell his subject." Many believe that they can afford to spend as much as 40 percent of the available teaching time in arousing a strong desire to know and only 60 percent in actual "instruction," and yet do a more successful job of teaching than if they had spent the entire time just stating the facts.

And this is especially true in teaching adults. *Adults can learn,* but, much more than with young people, they do not learn easily unless they are told just what the knowledge will do for them *now*—not at some time in the distant future.

Also, adults, especially mature adults, resent more strongly than do young people being "talked down" to in the all too typical teacher-pupil manner.

b. *Start with the known; lead into the unknown.* All teaching should start with that which is known. This at once captures the attention and gives you and those you are teaching a common starting point. For example, the description of a new screw machine may begin:

"The new machine is similar to, but has one important difference from the #47 which we are now using. You will remember that, on #47, when the operation gets to this point (holding up a piece of work or a blueprint and pointing to the place), the machine stops and the operator must turn the turret by hand. In the new design a cam has been introduced here (show large blueprint), etc."

c. *Teach the simple first and lead up to the complicated.* Any new subject or process is difficult at first. If you try to launch right into the more difficult parts of what you have to teach, you are likely to discourage the beginner. If you begin with the simpler parts and make sure that they are mastered before you attempt the complex, there will be much less discouragement.

Keep the learner progressing into the more complex, however, just as rapidly as his ability will permit, because, if the progress becomes too easy, he will be inclined to think that he has mastered the whole thing and that real effort is no longer necessary. In other words, try to gauge the speed of your teaching so that it constantly calls on the learner to give his best, but never goes beyond his ability.

d. *Keep your explanation to the point.* Avoid giving unrelated incidents and details, even if interesting, because the learner's attention will be taken off the main subject. Probably all of us are guilty at times of letting this or that remind us of something which happened when we were in the market the last time, or when we worked in a steel mill, or were camping last summer—incidents which, although interesting, do not really contribute anything of value and often take interest away from the subject being discussed.

It is, however, an excellent practice, wherever possible, to illustrate each more important point by a story, if the story actually makes the meaning clearer and causes the learner to remember the point.

e. *Give a reason for each step.* We remember anything much better if we know the reason why and, even in a simple process, there is always a reason why it is better to do it one way than another.

A second advantage in giving a reason is that any fact is more interesting when the learner knows the reason for it. Attention and all learning depend largely on interest.

A third advantage is that, if the learner knows the reason, he is much less likely to think some other way "just as good" and thus to get started in wrong methods.

The method used in presenting this principle of good teaching is an illustration of the principle itself. Three reasons are given why reasons should be given. It is for you to judge how much this increases the probability of your remembering and using this principle.

f. *Demonstrate by doing (or having done) correctly and exactly what the learner will later be asked to do.*

Be sure the learner can see every move and every part of the work being demonstrated.

Go as slowly as is necessary for every detail to be seen and understood. Often you will have done the particular thing you are teaching so frequently that it has become a habit for you to do it rapidly, and unless you are careful you will have a tendency to do it just as rapidly when showing the process to the learner. Try to avoid this.

And perform the operation the correct way only. Explain *briefly* why it is the correct way, and how other ways may cause confusion or damage, *but do not show how NOT to do the job.*

g. *Encourage discussion, especially questions.* One of the most important requirements for success in teaching, especially the type of teaching that you will usually be called upon to do, is to have the person being taught feel perfectly free to interrupt at any time to ask a question.

h. *Promptly after each operation has been explained and demonstrated to the learner, give him an opportunity to demonstrate the operation as if he were teaching you—making sure that he understands and explains to you the reasons for each step.*

This is probably the most important suggestion of all. When you explain just how to do a thing, even if your explanation is understood perfectly, the desired impression is established only slightly. Even when you demonstrate by doing the thing yourself, the impression still may be far from what you wish it to be. But when the learner is given a chance to do it and to explain it himself, the impression is greatly strengthened and, also, you have had an opportunity to make sure that your explanation and demonstration have been understood.

An amusing incident which occurred in our home some years ago illustrates the importance of this suggestion. A new maid, with no more than her share of intelligence, had been employed. She was supposed to go downstairs earlier than the family and, among other tasks, to bring in the milk. The side door had a thumb bolt and a regular lock. She was shown before she went to bed how both must be unlocked, and said that she understood.

The next morning the milk was not in; she could not unlock the door.

That night she was shown again most carefully just how to do it, and seemed to understand. The next morning the milk was still on the outside. The door was too much for Jane.

That evening my wife, who had been trained as a teacher, decided to apply some of her principles of teaching. She showed the maid carefully how it was done, then said, "Now, Jane, see if you can do it." After some fumbling and a little further coaching, Jane did it. The door was then locked, and Jane told to try again. She did much better, and after two or three trials she could do it quite well.

The next morning the milk was inside.

i. *Check from time to time to see how well the information is retained and used.* Every executive knows how important a part of his work is that represented by the word "follow-up." This is as true of teaching as of any other part of his work.

Having the employee do something that involves a use of the knowledge or ability gained is a better method of review than direct quizzing, because it shows not only that he possesses the necessary information, but also that he knows how to use it.

Your check should go beyond being assured that the person knows or even that he knows how to do; there should be some method of checking to see whether or not he is actually using the information in his everyday work.

As the executive you are not only responsible for what the person knows, you are also responsible for what he does with what he knows. And that, after all, is the best test of the excellence of any teaching.

j. *Use the same care, the same teaching technique, in giving instructions to an individual.* Too often, instructions to an individual are given much more hastily than would be the case if these instructions were given to a group. It is unfair to any employee to expect intelligent cooperation unless all necessary instructions are given fully, clearly, and with due regard for that person's feelings. The same basic principles that apply to all teaching apply to the giving of even the simplest instruction to an employee. Much need for discipline and for doing things over would be eliminated if instructions were always given this way, and in the end the supervisor's time would be saved. A simple formula for giving instructions to an individual is:

Tell how and why.

Do the thing yourself.

Let the learner do it.

Check frequently and tactfully.

7. Correct where correction is needed, but learn to do this in a friendly and helpful manner.

Correction is not the most pleasant task the executive is called upon to perform, but in that task lies one of his greatest opportunities for service both to his organization and to the people under his supervision.

Correction, real correction, corrects faulty performance by searching for and correcting the causes rather than by browbeating and threatening. It builds self-confidence and courage rather than fear, and enthusiastic cooperation rather than unwilling compliance.

The technique of this type of correction has "ten commandments." And in no phase of personnel supervision has a more definite, step-by-step technique been worked out or is it more essential to success that *all* of the "commandments" be obeyed.

a. *Try first to get all pertinent facts.* Too often we leap into an attempt at correction with an inadequate knowledge of the facts. When we do this, we usually limp out of the interview having accomplished little but to antagonize the person corrected.

Frequently, when we do obtain the facts, we find that what we had thought to be a case which needed discipline was really the result of poor teaching or poor placement on our part and, if anyone needed a reprimand, we did. So the first question should always be, "Have I done my part?"

b. *If possible, choose a place which is both private and quiet.* Correction should never be made in the presence of another employee, except such brief correction as may be necessary to stop, while it is being done, something which may cause injury to a person or damage to property.

Reasonable quiet also is important. If the interviewer and the person being corrected have to raise their voices to drown out other noise, there is a tendency for both to become excited.

c. *Always begin with a question.* There is probably no one rule in personnel supervision which is more absolute than the rule that every corrective interview should begin with a question. In my own experience of over 40 years, I can remember no exception.

Even in cases where we feel absolutely sure that a severe reprimand is justified, we lose nothing by opening with a question, and we may save ourselves embarrassment. Even when we feel absolutely sure, we are sometimes mistaken. We may feel, for example, that there can be no question about the guilt of a tool boy caught using a micrometer as a nutcracker, and that we are fully justified in starting the "corrective interview" in about the following manner:

"You ______ __________ blockhead, quit using that 'mike' for a nutcracker."

But the answer may be:

"I'm not so dumb as you think. This 'mike' is no good. It is an old one all sprung out of shape; the tool room foreman gave it to me to take home for my kid brother to play with. But it makes a swell nutcracker. Want to try it?"

Where then is our dignity, poise, prestige?

But if we begin with the question, "Why are you using a 'mike' to crack nuts?" we can answer the boy's explanation with the comment, "No, thank you, but that is a new one on me," and make our exit, dignity unimpaired.

On the other hand, if the boy's answer reveals that he is using a good mike, we can then quickly reach a decision as to whether he is ignorant or careless, and can go ahead either with instruction or reprimand, as the case demands.

But be careful to avoid the mistake Bill Towne made. He had attended a meeting in which we had discussed the importance of beginning each corrective interview with a question, so at the first opportunity he decided to apply the rule.

In his department there was a man, Tom Ashley, who was an excellent workman with long experience in performing a difficult operation necessary in the assembly of one of the machines manufactured by the company. But, recently, Tom had been absent quite frequently and often when he came in he looked somewhat "bleary-eyed" as if he had been drinking the night before.

So Bill decided to talk to Tom. He called him over to his desk, which was in a quiet corner of the department where no one could hear what was said. And he opened the interview with a question:

"Tom, why are you getting drunk almost every night and letting me down on the job the way you are? You know we are behind on our deliveries of Model 27, and that you are my best man on that model. Why don't you let drink alone and come to work every day?"

Tom explained to Bill, in none too friendly a manner, that he had not been drinking at all, but that his absence had been caused by the serious illness of his wife; that when he appeared on the job "bleary-eyed" the cause was loss of sleep; that he had not for years touched anything stronger to drink than coffee. And later investigation proved all these statements to be true.

Tom was a quiet sort of a fellow and didn't often lose his temper, but he did lose it that day. He told Bill just what he thought of him and then said he was going to the office for his time because he was through.

Bill succeeded in persuading Tom to stay, and as his wife's health improved his attendance became normal again.

At the next supervisors' meeting Bill told of his experience, and the group decided to add this to make this change in the rule: *Always begin with a question, but be sure that the question is not so worded that it is, itself, an accusation.*

They decided that it would have been much better had Bill opened his interview in some manner as this:

"Tom you have been absent quite a little lately, what's the trouble? Is there anything causing your absence we can help you with?"

d. *Give the person being corrected ample opportunity to talk.* Perhaps the employee has a real reason (or at least thinks he has) for his action, and if he gets a chance to tell this, you can more easily find a way to help him. He may wander away from the immediate subject, but such wanderings are often more revealing of the real cause of the difficulty than would be the answers to specific questions. Do not hurry the interview. Listen attentively.

e. *Consider carefully all of the evidence.* You have, before the interview, gathered all the information you could. You have, in the interview, heard the employee's side of the question and have tried to look at it in the light of his opinions and feelings. You are now in a position to decide what you believe to have been the real cause of the error or difficulty. When this is done, the hardest part of the task of correction is completed; decision as to the nature and extent of correction necessary is relatively easy.

It may be that the new evidence will cause you to decide that no correction at all is necessary. If so, you should close the interview promptly and pleasantly. If you have begun the interview with the right kind of a question the employee need never know that correction was in your mind, and nothing will have been taken away from his interest in his work, his self-confidence, and his feeling that he is being treated fairly.

f. *Fit the method of correction to the individual.* Many executives use exactly the same approach for every individual. This is poor technique. One person may be sensitive, and a blunt approach may merely antagonize and hurt him, making impossible any real teaching. And, after all, teaching is usually the real purpose of the corrective interview.

For another person a blunt, straight-from-the-shoulder statement of his fault and what he must do to correct it may be necessary to get results, although this is not often true.

There is one important point to be kept constantly in mind—the purpose of correction is to correct. Punishment is definitely not the purpose, although some disciplinary action may at times be necessary.

The securing of a positive admission from the employee that he is wrong and is sorry is not necessary, if the supervisor feels that the employee has admitted this *to himself* and will discontinue the undesirable behavior.

The purpose of correction is to correct—to make right that which was wrong—nothing else.

g. *Maintain your own calmness regardless of the employee's attitude.* It is important that the interview be kept on as impersonal a basis as possible. The moment you let the corrective interview descend to the plane of argument it has lost its effectiveness. The less any executive thinks or says about his power, his dignity, his feelings, his prerogatives, and the more he thinks and says about job standards, the more successful the interview will be.

The person interviewed may even make some uncomplimentary

remarks concerning you, and in this case it will be difficult indeed to eliminate personal feelings. You should always, however, endeavor to think only in terms of job requirements and how the person has fallen short in meeting these requirements, rather than of any affront to your own feelings.

h. *Close pleasantly; restore self-confidence.* When the person has indicated what you believe to be a sincere desire to correct his fault, and the necessary directions as to how to go about it have been given, the interview should be closed.

His courage and self-confidence must be restored and his enthusiasm renewed. It is well to close the interview by mentioning his good qualities, and assuring him that you are certain that he will have no difficulty in eliminating the one thing which is holding him back, if he will really try. Offer to help in any way you can, and invite him to come back to see you at any time to discuss his progress.

i. *Follow up with a second interview, if necessary.* After any corrective interview, the employee's performance should be watched, but unobtrusively. If the correction has not proven fully effective, the employee should be sent for again. A good opening sentence then might be: "I just sent for you to ask you if there were any points about our talk last week which were not clear. As I remember it, you said that you were going to," etc.

This approach, which brings in the thought that the person may have misunderstood the first interview, allows him, even at this late date, to correct his wrong attitude without sacrificing his dignity.

j. *Do not use correction too often.* Do not let correction descend to the level of nagging.

Attitude toward the employee with a grievance. In the experience of everyone responsible for guiding and supervising the efforts of others there will be cases of people who find it difficult to adjust themselves properly either to the job or to the group with which they work. They come to the executive frequently with complaints of one kind or another, or their associates complain about them.

The executive's success or failure in handling these problem people will depend on the attitude he takes toward them and their grievances more than on any other one thing.

First, there must be a real interest in the employee's problem and a genuine desire to settle the complaint to his full satisfaction if this is at all possible.

Second, there must be a feeling of *actual gratitude* for the opportunity given to correct a cause of dissatisfaction, instead of resentment or annoyance. And this feeling must be made evident by the executive's manner. The executive has real reason to be grateful, because no grievance can be satisfactorily adjusted unless it is known, and there is nothing worse for morale than a pent-up grievance.

Third, there must be full understanding that the person who comes to an executive with a grievance often has "boiled inside" for some time before he built up courage to come. As a result, without intending to be so, he may be somewhat untactful in how he presents his case. If the executive maintains his calm and friendly attitude he will have a much better chance to locate the real cause of the grievance and to correct it.

Fourth, there must be full appreciation of the fact that the employee may be sincere in the belief that he is right, even though it is obvious to any unbiased observer that he is wrong.

And finally, there must be a sincere desire and effort to find the real cause of the employee's inability to adjust to the work situation and to help him to correct whatever may be the trouble.

An executive of long experience once remarked to me that it was surprising how often people who had in one way or another been his "problem cases" turned out to be his best people, in many instances becoming successful executives themselves. So it is worth whatever time, effort, and self-control it may take.

8. Give to the people under your supervision as full a part as is practicable in planning those things which affect their working conditions.

If it is at all practicable, each situation which may necessitate any change in working conditions, especially any undesirable change, should be discussed with those to be affected. And this discussion should not be merely in advance of the change itself but *before any decision is made as to just what change will be necessary.* The employees should have the situation explained to them and their suggestions requested as to the solution which will cause the least hardship all around. Often employees will set for themselves a more rigorous schedule than you would have suggested.

9. Have your organizational set-up such that there is no confusion in anyone's mind as to his exact duties, responsibilities, and authority.

The responsibilities assigned to each unit and to each person should be specific, clear-cut, and fully understood not only by the persons themselves, but also by all other persons in the organization.

Responsibility for the performance of any function should carry with it the authority necessary to perform that function.

Self Rating on Ability or Potential Ability to Supervise People

Knowledge of the job and expertness in doing it were for many years the sole qualifications necessary for promotion to positions of responsibility.

That is rapidly becoming a thing of the past.

Top managements are putting more and more emphasis on what they believe would be the ability each candidate for promotion has to win the full cooperation of any group he will immediately or may later supervise.

How would *you* measure up in this competition?

Following the general directions and using the rating scale given at the close of Chapter 3, answer each question by writing in the space provided the letter or letters which will indicate your carefully considered opinion of the extent to which you actually do the things described in the question.

Fairness

What was your rating of yourself on *Fairness* following Chapter 3? ______

How careful are you, after reaching a decision, always to make sure that the persons affected understand the reasons and are convinced that these reasons are sound and fair? ______

How careful are you when talking to applicants to make no statements that might be misconstrued as promises? ______

After considering these new questions, how do you rate yourself on *Fairness?* [ ]

Selection

How careful and systematic are you in determining and considering the duties and requirements of the job to be filled both when selecting new employees and when transferring someone to a new job? ______

How regularly do you prepare a "selection plan" in writing when selecting a new employee or planning a transfer? ______

To what extent do you "ask questions which call for narrative statements" when interviewing applicants? ______

Taking into account these answers and a review of your actual success, how do you rate yourself on *Selection?* ☐

Introduction of the New Employee to His Job

When you are very busy at the time a new employee is brought to you, how nearly is your manner of receiving him like that of Jim Swain rather than that of Bill Hastings? ☐

Showing Your Employees That Their Efforts Are Appreciated

How carefully and consistently do you look for and comment pleasantly about things that are worthy of comment? ☐

How carefully and even persistently do you make an effort to secure salary increases for people under your supervision who deserve it? ☐

Training

To what extent do you have a regular and carefully planned training program in the department you supervise? ☐

How fully, in any training personally done by you, are you careful to apply the ten suggestions given in this chapter? ☐

Correction

How carefully and consistently do you regularly "obey" the "ten commandments" of correction? ☐

Part in Planning

How regularly do you give to the people under your supervision as full a part as is possible in planning in advance things which will affect their working conditions? ☐

Where this is not practicable, how careful are you to explain in advance the reasons for any change? ☐

After considering carefully all of your answers to these questions, but not necessarily striking an average, rate yourself on how fully you believe you are doing the things which should get real cooperation from the people you supervise. ☐

8

HOW TO MEET AND PROFIT FROM DISAPPOINTMENTS

THE EXACT MANNER IN WHICH WE HAVE MET DISappointments throughout our lives and are now meeting them in our day-to-day living has a greater effect on our success and happiness than most of us realize, possibly greater than any other one thing.

Disappointments will come to all of us, no matter how hard we try to avoid them. We need not let them cause any lasting bad effect, however, and often we can make them foundation stones for even greater success and happiness.

But disappointments, however we look at them, are unpleasant. They do hurt at the time. And the more any disappointment takes away from the all-important sense of importance and worthiness we all prize so highly and protect so ardently, the more keenly will it be felt.

Sometimes the hurt may be so great that we must find a way, not always a healthful way, to alleviate the pain. Any long continued sense of personal inferiority or feeling of shame seems to be unendurable. That all-important feeling of personal worthwhileness must be restored. If this is not done in a normal, fact-facing, healthful manner, it will be done in some less desirable way. *It must be done.*

Whenever we find that, in some way, we have been prevented from doing something we have desired most strongly to do, or have made a failure of what we had hoped would be a triumph, or have had our "feelings hurt" by some act or some inattention of a friend or associate, there are two ways we can meet the situation.

We may, and of course we should, endeavor to find the true facts as to why the thing happened and, facing these facts squarely, work out a solution which takes them fully into account.

But the facts which one must face after almost any seriously disappointing or embarrassing experience or after having done something which, deep down in his heart, he knows to be unworthy of him, are not, as a rule, pleasant ones. The ego has usually been brought to a low point by the experience itself, and it is indeed difficult to face facts which may bring it even lower. Of course, in the long run, the feeling that one has done the courageous thing in facing up to the truth will more effectively restore the ego to its normal state than any fact-evading method, but, when the ego is low, it is much easier and, for the time being, certainly much more pleasant just to evade the facts.

So, much too often, we all choose the easier way and construct "defense mechanisms" as psychologists call those methods one may use to "defend" his ego and to restore it to something like its normal level without the painful necessity of having to correct or to admit any of his faults, even to himself.

Some Fact-Facing Methods of Adjustment to Disappointments and Embarrassment

Perhaps the first step should be to assume quite frankly that we probably do occasionally try to explain away disappointments and embarrassments by excuses which are only part of the real cause—often only a small part. Practically every one does.

Indeed, so common is this practice that J. Pierpont Morgan is credited with having said that everyone has two reasons for almost everything he does, a *good* one and the *real* one.

The next step should be to begin at once to make it a practice after each disappointment or embarrassment to ask ourselves these four questions and to answer each as impersonally and as objectively as we can:

1. *Was there any lack of thoroughness?* Probably more than to any other one cause, failures and the resulting disappointments, both in business and in social life, are due to lack of careful planning and preparation and meticulous care in carrying out the plan.
2. *Was there any lack of tact?* Were we so busy doing things which, to us, seemed to contribute more directly to success that we did not take the time to say and do the little things which please people? Especially, have we always been careful to thank those who have helped us?
3. *Was there any lack of good judgment?* Were our goals well chosen? This was discussed more fully in Chapter 2.
4. *Did we expect too much?* A realistic view of what we may reasonably expect in the way of rewards and especially in attention and praise may frequently save us from "hurt feelings," and there are few if any forms of disappointment which are more painful.

When we have had the courage to examine fairly and impersonally the facts, we will, as a rule, reach the conclusion that a part at least of most disappointments has been some fault or lack of ability on our part and that the disappointment might have been avoided had we acted differently.

This done, there are at least three satisfactory and emotionally healthful ways in which we may remedy the situation and restore any impairment the ego may have suffered:[1]

1. *We may try again.*

If, after calmy reviewing and weighing all of the circumstances surrounding the situation, we decide that success is reasonably possible in the same field of endeavor, we may first eliminate as fully as we can the things which caused the original disappointment and then wholeheartedly try again and again until we win. This, where possible, is the best solution.

If, however, we decide that this is impossible or impracticable, we have at least two other fact-facing and effective courses of action we may follow.

2. *We may try to find a satisfactory and socially acceptable substitute activity.*

Quite often, when the satisfaction of some fundamental desire is prevented by seemingly insurmountable conditions, the disappointment may be compensated for by finding a socially acceptable substitute activity which restores that all-important feeling of personal worthiness.

And there will have been *true compensation* if the person fully accepts the new activity as a satisfactory substitute, with no bitterness and no daydreaming about "what might have been."

Often, with some careful thought, we may find a truly compensating activity closely related to the thing which we have been prevented from doing.

One example of how this may be done is found in the case of a young friend of mine who met with and mastered a truly serious disappointment.

---

[1] Emotionally healthful ways are those which are not motivated primarily by fear, hate, jealousy, desire for revenge, or other self-centered and unhealthful emotions.

Slim Brown played several musical instruments well and, up until he was about 18 years old, had been able to sing quite well, too. It had been his ambition to play and sing in a good dance orchestra, but a serious throat ailment had left him with a somewhat raucous voice which was more amusing than musical.

He did, however, get a job in one of the best dance bands in the city and was doing quite well, but he still wanted the applause which goes to the man who puts his instrument down and steps out and sings.

He was talking to his mother about all of this one day.

"Son," she said, "your problem reminds me of something my father once told me which helped me so much that I am surprised that I have not told you about it before. I had gone to him with some serious disappointment and he said, 'Always try to make lemonade of your lemons.' He explained, that if you just take a lemon alone and bite into it you get something most unpleasant, but if you 'dress up' the lemon a little with some sugar and water and a little ice you have lemonade—and who doesn't like a good cool glass of lemonade? 'Disappointments are like lemons,' he said, 'they often have great possibilities for good in them.'

"Now your disappointment—your lemon—is your voice, but maybe even that has some good qualities. It is strong, it has considerable range, and when you try to do so you can make it sound quite comical, if that has any advantage."

"Yes, it does, Mother," Slim said enthusiastically, "and I think you have given me an idea. There is a new song about a big bear and a little rabbit. The bear says (deep voice), the little rabbit replies (high squeaky voice), and all of that. I cannot sing but my voice *is* funny. It can go low and it can go high and squeaky. I'll get Jim to fix an arrangement so I can make lemonade out of that lemon."

"Maybe I can add a little sugar to your lemonade," his mother added. "How would it do to have some sort of headgear—great big head for the big bear, little head with long ears for the little rabbit—and then change rapidly as you take each part."

The idea worked splendidly. As each new novelty song came out, Slim's mother and later his wife worked out novelty ideas in headdress. And Slim became one of the most popular singers in town. He had made lemonade of his lemons—and very good lemonade too.

We can do the same with many of our disappointments—with our lemons.

In the future, when a disappointment does come, we should not take time to worry about it. Rather we should start at once with the much more pleasant task of figuring out just how we can make the whole thing work out to our advantage instead of disadvantage.

It is surprising, if we will really try, how often we can do this, how often we can make lemonade of our lemons.

Sometimes, however, it may be necessary for us to turn our energies to a somewhat different field but one in which we can *win satisfactions which are similar,* like the boy who found football impossible and took up tennis and golf and thus eliminated any feeling of inferiority which failure to make the football team may have given him.

Or, even if there is no opportunity for us to do this, we may use our energies in an entirely different but equally worthy field and win satisfaction there, thus compensating for the disappointment, sometimes so fully that when we look back years later we will realize that what seemed to be a misfortune was really a blessing. For example, a boy prevented by lameness from winning recognition in athletics may study to be a doctor and help thousands to avoid the disease which made him lame.

3. We may just accept the disappointment gracefully.

Occasionally, it may even be wise to admit frankly that we just cannot have some one thing which we have wanted and to decide that we shall be happy with what we can have and can do and, further, that there will be no regrets and no bitterness. Of course, this method of adjustment to disappointments should not be used too often. It should never be used when careful and courageous analysis shows that success is reasonably possible and the happiness success would bring to our families and to ourselves is worth the effort and sacrifice necessary to achieve that success.

These and similar fact-facing ways of meeting disappointments build sound, well-adjusted, and happy personalities.

And it should always be remembered that there is nothing harmful, physically or emotionally, in any feeling of inferiority we may have in some one or more fields of endeavor, provided we are making a real effort in an intelligent and emotionally healthful manner to compensate for it by accomplishment in some other field.

In fact, many students of human nature believe that most great achievements in any field spring from a feeling of inferiority in some other field.

Self Rating on How Well You Meet Disappointments

Using the same system you have used in the preceding chapters, rate yourself on the following questions:

1. When serious disappointments come, to what extent do you believe that you regularly "face the facts" and try to find a sound and emotionally healthful way to remedy the situation? ______

2. How fully do you believe yourself to be free from the all-too-common tendency to stress too much, even in your own thinking, the part of the reason for the disappointment which was "not your fault"? ______

9

HOW TO HANDLE YOUR WORK LOAD EFFICIENTLY

THERE ARE AT LEAST THREE WAYS IN WHICH PRACtically all of us—executive and minor clerk alike—often waste time: (1) by actually doing nothing; (2) by doing things which are completely or largely useless; (3) by doing useful work in a haphazard, unplanned, or otherwise inefficient manner.

And in the case of executives—from president to first-line supervisor—there is, also, an even more seriously harmful way in which time is often wasted. It is by doing so much work that someone less skilled could and should do that it is impossible to find time to do properly highly important work which, actually, no one else can do so satisfactorily.

Delegation of authority and responsibility is the solution. This will be discussed later.

Improving Personal Efficiency

No one wants to be a machine, clicking off each activity of the day with perfect precision, and never "wasting" a moment with what he considers trivialities.

We do not like such people. And, as a matter of fact, they

are seldom really successful either in business or in the home.

But practically all of us do waste more of our time than we should—probably more than we realize. For most of us, a sensible application of well-established principles of personal efficiency will enable us to eliminate much of this waste and will not cause any risk of our getting into the "efficiency-nut" classification.

A Four-Step Plan for Studying and Improving Work Methods[1]

Few of us realize how inefficiently we actually do many things until we apply to our own operations the four steps usually applied by practically all efficiency engineers when undertaking to improve work methods.

Step 1. Prepare in writing a detailed, step-by-step description of exactly how the job is being done now.

Familiar as we all are with how we do each job, it might seem to be unnecessary to write the description in full detail, but such is not the case. There is something about writing down each small thing we do which makes the unnecessary things stand out like "sore thumbs."

During World War II, when a group of us were in Atlanta attending an institute for instructors in the Job Methods Training Course, we were asked to make a "breakdown" (as this type of job description is called) of some job exactly as we did it. Since we were in a hotel and not carrying out our normal activities, several of us prepared breakdowns of our shaving in the morning.

I was, at that time, using shaving cream, brush, and safety razor.

---

[1] Largely adapted from the Job Methods Training Course of the Training-Within-Industry Program of the War Manpower Commission which was used extensively in industry during World War II. The author was one of the instructors in this course.

I wish I had saved that breakdown. I believe it would win a prize in any competition. But the prize, I fear, would be for comedy rather than efficiency.

Try it yourself some morning. I doubt if you can equal my record for wasted time, but you may be surprised to see how many wasted motions there are, even in this job you do practically every morning of the year.

It will be good practice, also, to make a breakdown of some job you do around the house, such as fixing a leaking faucet.

After some such practice you will be better prepared to make helpful breakdowns of your regular work or that of people under your supervision.

But always remember to list *all* details, using a separate line for each small thing done. Any grouping of several details on one line will make much more difficult the analysis of the breakdown to determine which details are unnecessary or could be done in a better way.

The employees who will use any improved method should, if practicable, work with you in the development of that method.

Step 2. Question every detail.

These questions should be asked concerning each separate detail of the breakdown:

1. WHY is this detail performed? What purpose does it accomplish, and is this purpose a necessary one?
2. WHO should do this part of the job? WHERE should it be done? WHEN should it be done? Can it be done more economically and just as satisfactorily by someone else and can he do it better at some other time and place?
3. HOW should it be done? Can the present method be improved upon? Are there unnecessary or needlessly difficult and awkward motions? Are all materials and tools in the places where they can be most easily reached by the opera-

tor? Are they so placed that he picks them up naturally in the position in which they will be used?

Practice has shown that it is best to ask the "why" questions concerning *all of the details,* before asking the other questions. The purpose of asking these questions first is to determine what details may be eliminated.

Next, "who, where, and when" should be asked concerning each step. If a carefully considered answer to any question makes some change in method seem desirable, a brief note should be made describing the proposed change.

Finally, the "how" questions are asked in an endeavor to find the best way to do each necessary detail.

Step 3. Work out and write a breakdown of the proposed new method.

From notes made in answering the questions, prepare a complete breakdown of the proposed new method. Review this breakdown, asking the same questions, and make any further changes.

Step 4. Put the improved method into operation.

First, secure any necessary approval from higher executives. Second, explain the new method to the employees who will use it. Third, put it into operation, watching most carefully to be sure everything is working as planned.

And be constantly on the alert for further improvement.

A Record and Analysis of a Day's Activities

I am sure you will find it helpful, also, as I have, to make as accurate a record as you can of just what you do each half hour of one or two days, especially, how much of each half hour you would consider wasted time.

But first a word of caution. While making this rather detailed record in the manner described later, try to act as naturally as you can. Do not look at your watch too often. Make entries only when you can do so privately.

The reason for this caution is that any analysis for self-improvement can be made much more frankly and objectively if it is done without anyone else knowing exactly what you are doing.

Absolute accuracy is not essential. This will not be a split-second time and motion study. For the record to be useful, however, it should be as accurate as possible. The recording of the time spent on each activity and how much of that time you think was wasted should be made all through the day as nearly each half hour as possible.

You may find it to be quite difficult, however, to get a record of your time as you *regularly and naturally spend it.* The very fact that you are trying to notice and to include in your record how much of your time you actually spend on useless activities will definitely cause you to spend less time than usual on such activities. This cannot be avoided, but try to make the record as true a picture as you can of your normal behavior. You will be the only person who sees it.

The Record. On letter-size sheets of paper which you can fold easily to carry in your pocket, prepare as many copies as you will need of a chart about like that shown on the next page.

As promptly as you can after each half hour, record what your activities have been and, in the right-hand column show the time in minutes you believe you have "wasted."

What is "time wasted"? The answer is: (1) time, not actually needed for rest, in which you are doing nothing, (2) time used in doing something which is completely or largely useless, and (3) time wasted while doing useful work because the work is done in an inefficient manner.

Period	Date ____________ WHAT YOU DID	Minutes Wasted
To 7:30		
To 8:00		
To 8:30		
To 9:00		
To 9:30		
To 10:00		
To 10:30		
To 11:00		
To 11:30		
To 12:00		
To 12:30		
To 1:00		
To 1:30		
To 2:00		
To 2:30		
To 3:00		
To 3:30		
To 4:00		
To 4:30		
To 5:00		
To 5:30		
To 6:00		

__________Minutes Wasted __________% of Total

But what should be considered "completely or largely useless"? A brief exchange of friendly comments on the part of associates certainly is not wasted time because it helps to build mutual good will. However, lengthy exchange of stories either in the office or on "coffee break" certainly is wasted time.

Healthful recreation is not wasted time nor is taking time for a quiet, unhurried lunch. But excessive time for either purpose probably is.

Each person must decide for himself where to draw the line between useful and useless.

There will, of course, not be time to make a detailed analysis of each thing you do to decide how much of your time while doing useful work is wasted because of inefficiency. For this record and analysis, an informal estimate should be used.

At the close of the day the minutes wasted should be added up, and percent of total time computed.

This analysis is, of course, not recommended as a permanent plan. It can be used profitably for the first one or two days and, after that, about one day each month.

There is not space in one chapter to discuss adequately the subject of improving work methods. For those who wish to study the subject somewhat more fully the following book is recommended:

Barnes, Ralph M., *Work Methods Manual,* New York: John Wiley & Sons, 1944. A short and decidedly practical discussion of the principles of work organization and motion economy, written especially for supervisors. Each principle and rule is illustrated by examples.

Delegation of Responsibility and Authority

George Mitchell had been with the Evans Company, wholesalers of hardware and mill supplies, for 40 years. When he started, he was the entire office force. But the business grew and by 1950 he was treasurer and comptroller with a force of 54 people working under him.

For several years the son of the original Mr. Evans, who had become general manager, tried to persuade Mr. Mitchell to give more responsibility and authority to John Simpson, a capable young accountant who had been with the organization about eight years.

Mr. Mitchell almost flatly refused. He said that Mr. Simpson was a "fine boy and a good bookkeeper," but that he wasn't ready yet to assume responsibility. He would think about it as soon as the busy season was over. It went on this way for two or three years. Mr. Mitchell was still making every decision and personally dictating practically every letter. And during the busy season he usually worked until nine or ten o'clock every night.

Then what everyone expected and feared happened He suffered a heart attack. He was out about ten weeks and the doctor said that it would be extremely foolish for him ever again to try to work too hard.

Mr. Evans did the only thing he could do. He put Mr. Simpson in full charge of the accounting department and appointed as credit manager a man who had done that work for several years —under Mr. Mitchell's usual detailed supervision, of course.

But he did this with considerable fear and trembling because he realized that it had been impossible for him to take all of the steps which should always be taken before there is complete delegation of responsibility and authority.

But, fortunately, it did work out well.

When Mr. Mitchell returned, he retained the title of Treasurer, was assigned an office in the executive suite and, with only a secretary under his supervision, personally handled the important fiscal matters and the executive payroll.

But what are the steps which should be taken in properly effecting satisfactory delegation of responsibility and authority?

1. Teach EVERYONE to make decisions.

One large firm which enjoyed extremely rapid but thoroughly healthy growth over a period of many years has, from the beginning, carried out all of the usually accepted personnel practices.

These have, of course, played an important part in enabling the organization to grow as it has without, so far as I know, it ever having been necessary to bring in new employees in anything but relatively minor positions.

But there has been one practice, started by the founder of the company, about which one seldom, if ever, reads in books on personnel management, but which I believe has contributed as much to the total success of the company as did any of the more formal plans.

It was the practice, throughout the organization of always requiring *any person,* from mail clerk to vice-president, whenever he came to his chief to ask how to carry out any project or meet any situation, *first* to tell how he thought the job should be done.

The mail clerk was not permitted to ask, "How must this be mailed?" He had to say, "I believe we should mail this parcel post because—" or some similar recommendation.

And the vice-president, who incidentally might have started as a mail clerk, would have followed this practice for so many years that, before he went in to see the president to ask his opinion on some new project, he would have made thorough investigation and have a carefully prepared recommendation.

This practice does two things, and both are most important to the success of any program of delegation of authority and responsibility.

First, it trains everyone in the organization to think for himself and to reach decisions.

Second, it gives to every executive a sound basis for forming a judgment as to the intelligence, initiative, and judgment of the people under his supervision.

2. Decide what and to whom to delegate.

No real executive can, or even wants to escape from the hard work, the responsibility, or even the frequent high pressure involved in making and acting quickly on important decisions. There is an element of excitement in this which gives one something akin to the thrill that hunting big game gives to the sportsman. The executive does not want to give this up, nor should he do so, because no one else can do this most important part of his job as well as he can.

But the zest for this normally interesting part of the executive's work will fade away if his time is so completely taken up with routine duties that there is almost a feeling of "I wish they would leave me alone" when some important non-routine duty must be performed or decision made.

And too often he may be forced to perform the duty or make the decision without giving the time and unworried thinking so necessary for the quality of performance of which he is really capable.

Every executive should and, for real success, *must* delegate to carefully selected assistants responsibility and authority necessary for them to carry out enough of his more routine duties so that he will definitely have time for creative thinking, for making unhurried decisions on important matters, for adequate recreation, and for a good family life.

The first rule to follow in deciding what to delegate is that the power to make and carry out decisions should be as close to the actual operations as is practicable, taking into account the ability of the assistant to whom the authority is to be delegated and the seriousness of the consequences of an error.

Another rule which has much merit is to delegate as much authority as is needed for successful operation of the functions the assistant supervises, but no more.

A third and most important rule is that the exact scope of the authority given to each person should be clearly defined, preferably in writing.

3. Delegate authority somewhat gradually.

Unless the executive has thorough knowledge of the ability of the assistant to whom authority is being delegated, the scope of that authority should be definitely limited at first.

Then as the assistant shows that he has the ability to use the authority wisely, the scope of his authority should be increased until he has the full authority needed for successful carrying out of the functions he supervises.

Some organizations set up the exact authority according to title. There is, for example, a statement of duties for a foreman which specifies what the foreman may do himself and what he must refer to higher authority. The same powers and the same limitations apply to *all* foremen.

But all foremen are not alike either in ability or in experience. It would be dangerous to allow the newly appointed foreman the same authority in every phase of his work that might safely be given to a foreman with years of successful experience.

Armstrong Cork Company, with over 2,000 supervisors in plants widely separated geographically, has developed a plan as part of the training program which keeps each supervisor continuously informed as to exactly what *his* "degree of authority" is in each of his responsibilities.

There are, in general, three levels of authority:

Class 1. Full authority to take the necessary action in carrying out the responsibility without consulting or reporting to the superior.

Class 2. Full authority to take the necessary action, but the superior is to be informed of the action taken.

Class 3. Authority is limited. The supervisor is expected to present his recommendation to his superior and may not take action until a decision is reached.

Policy, past practice, and personal qualifications are all taken into account in determining the degree of authority given to each supervisor in each of his responsibilities.

It is obviously desirable to have these working relationships clearly understood at the outset.

To accomplish this the superior discusses in detail each assigned responsibility with each supervisor and records on a "Degree of Authority Form" which of the three levels of authority he wishes the supervisor to exercise in the carrying out of *each* of his responsibilities. A copy of the form, so marked, is given to the supervisor.

The supervisor's superior discusses the form with the supervisor at regular intervals, making whatever changes in the degrees of authority seem justified.

I believe some similar plan could be worked out for all levels of authority and, if properly explained, would be welcomed by those executives to whom responsibility and authority is being delegated.

This is true because there are few things more frustrating to any executive than to be given the responsibility for carrying out a certain assignment, but not to know just how much authority he has.

4. Keep informed as to how well the duties are being performed.

When an executive delegates to an assistant the authority and responsibility for the performance of any duties, he does not in any way lessen his own responsibility and accountability to his chief for the correct performance of those duties.

It is most important, therefore, that he not only select and train most carefully the assistant to whom the duties are to be delegated, but also that he provide some way of keeping in touch all along with how well the work is being done. And the information should reach him promptly so that any needed correction can be made before there are serious consequences.

Three methods of getting this information are commonly used —reports, meetings, and informal conferences.

Reports should give, as frequently as is necessary, statistical data which will indicate the "health" of the activity. There should be, also, a place for comment where the assistant can add any significant information not included in the data.

Regular meetings of all of the assistants reporting directly to the executive are important. Recommendations of one section head may affect the operations of another section.

Informal conferences with individual assistants are also important. If the attitude of the executive is friendly and helpful, the assistant will not hesitate to report some unsatisfactory condition which may be just developing and ask for advice before any report indicating the condition would normally reach the executive.

And the executive should seldom tell the assistant how to correct the condition. In a friendly way he should help the assistant to reach his own decision.

One day, several years ago, I was sitting outside the office of Samuel W. Reyburn, then president of the Associated Dry Goods Corporation, waiting to report on some work I was doing for him.

One of the store presidents came out of the office and stopped for a moment to chat. One thing he said I shall always remember. It was, "I have come to see Mr. Reyburn many times to ask questions about how I should handle certain situations. He has never yet told me what to do, but in every case I have known what was the correct solution before I left his office."

The more fully this can be said about any executive the more will his assistants always feel that they can come to him with any problem which is bothering them, and *the less frequently will they need to come.*

Self Rating on How Efficiently You Handle Your Work Load

1. To what extent do you feel that you have achieved a satisfactory degree of progress in actually using the four-step plan for studying and improving the tasks you do personally? ______

2. Same, in the work under your supervision? ______

3. How well satisfied are you with the progress you have made in cutting down wasted time in the activities of your normal day? ______

4. If you are in a supervisory or higher position, how satisfactory do you consider your progress in selecting and training qualified employees who can accept delegated responsibility when the need arises? ______

5. How well satisfied are you with your progress in actually delegating your less important duties so that you have more time to perform properly your more important duties? ______

10

HOW TO WRITE EFFECTIVE LETTERS AND REPORTS

ONE OF THE MOST IMPRESSIVE AND LASTINGLY EFFECtive lessons I ever had in the art of letter writing came from a man with only a limited education and certainly no training in writing letters.

William Smith had applied for a loan. After the necessary investigation had been completed a letter was sent to him approving the application.

But, probably, it was full of such expressions as "the above captioned application," "collateral," and "liquidate the indebtedness."

In a few days this reply was received:

> Dear Mr. Jones:
> I wants the truf. What I wants to know is is I gone to git the lone or is I aint.
> William Smith

When we first saw this letter it was passed around as a good joke, but gradually the lesson sank in. Here, probably, was a much better letter than the one which had been sent to him. In fact, it was a masterpiece of naturalness, simplicity, clearness, correctness and completeness of information, and conciseness. And I should probably add, of over-all effectiveness.

William Smith had taught all of us a much needed lesson in letter writing.

Of course, it would be inexcusable for any office to send out letters with misspelled words or mistakes in grammar. There should be regular training of dictators and stenographers and frequent spot checks to prevent any such errors.

But I wonder if, in our concern about spelling, grammar, and whether this or that setup is better than another (important as these things are), we do not sometimes overlook some of the requirements which are even more important in making our letters effective in the actual accomplishment of their intended purpose.

Another and an equally impressive lesson, applicable to both letter writing and public speaking, came from one of the most beautifully educated men I have ever known.

For several years we lived in a suburb of New York. Once each year a famous bishop lectured in a small church in our neighborhood. We always attended and enjoyed the lectures very much. And each time, as we were walking home, one or the other of us would comment, "Have you ever before known anyone who has such marvelous command of the English language. It was truly beautiful."

But I cannot remember that either of us ever commented on *what he had said.* I doubt if we remembered. We were, I fear, too entranced by the beautiful flow of language to remember.

This reminds me of something a French writer once said to the effect that "Good style is like a clear pane of glass through which one sees objects without realizing that the glass is there."

Why Do We Write Letters?

Whenever we write any letter we should keep constantly in mind a two-fold purpose.

First, there is some definite objective we wish to accomplish. We may wish to ask for information about something, to explain some policy or practice, to sell something, to buy something, to collect an account, to notify a customer that a request is being granted or is not granted, or any of many other specific things.

Second, we want always to build good will for our organizations, certainly never to say anything which will tear down whatever good will exists.

It is surprising, when we think of it, how large a part of all of the contacts with its customers made by any large business, even a retail store, is made through letters. So it is quite probable that, to a much larger extent than most of us realize, the good will of customers toward *our* organizations depends on the quality of the letters *we,* you and I, write.

What Is a Good Letter?

A good letter will have three parts, each with a specific purpose, in harmony with the two-fold purpose of the entire letter:

First, there should be a brief and pleasing opening which definitely identifies the subject and shows that the writer is interested in the problems and welfare of the person to whom the letter is sent.

Second, all necessary information should be stated accurately, clearly, tactfully, and with the real purpose of the letter always clearly in mind.

Third, a clear, concise, and tactful statement of the exact conclusion and, if appropriate, exactly what the writer of the letter would like the recipient to do.

And all three parts of the letter should be:

1. *Natural,* having much of the informality and friendliness of conversation.

2. *Simple and clear,* so that the person who receives the letter will have no doubt as to the exact meaning.

3. *Correct and complete in the information given.* There is little use in stating information clearly unless it is absolutely correct in every detail and all essential information is included.

4. *Pleasing in tone,* showing real interest in the problems of the person to whom we are writing and our desire to help.

5. *Concise,* using words enough to convey our exact meaning, our friendly feeling, and our desire to be helpful, but no more.

6. *Correct in grammar and spelling,* since such errors may have a bad effect on the reader's confidence in the quality of service our organization is capable of rendering.

7. *Neat and correct in typing and setup.* There is probably no one setup which can be called the one and only correct one, but in general, anything decidedly unusual and spectacular should be avoided.

8. *Effective as a whole.* This, of course, is what counts. Those who receive and read our letters seldom analyze them. They are pleased or displeased with the letter as a whole and, as a result, with the writer and the organization he represents.

Naturalness

Perhaps the best way we can achieve the naturalness of style we find today in the letters which are the most effective is to follow this simple rule:

Write as you would talk—but not quite so.

What we really want in a letter is the freshness and informality of conversational English, but without the carelessness in grammar and sentence structure or the tendency to verbosity and rambling all too common in most informal conversations.

Probably the style we would use in a carefully planned long-distance telephone conversation comes nearer than anything else to the style desirable in a letter. Here is an example:

Mr. Williams wrote for directions as to how to make a certain adjustment on a piece of machinery he had purchased. He received a reply from the manufacturer, but there was one point on which he felt that he needed somewhat fuller information and he needed it promptly. So he decided to telephone.

Both to save expense and to be sure he got all of the information he needed, he planned rather carefully what he would say, then placed a call for the writer of the letter. Here is about what he said when he was connected with the person called:

"Mr. Wilson, this is Samuel Williams of ———, Florida. I appreciate very much your letter of November 23 telling me just how to make the adjustment for cutting the heavy grass of this area with your L 47 mower, but there is one added thing I need to know. When the gears are set as you direct in your letter, would it be safe to operate at three-fourths or even full speed?

"It works fine at half speed, but if I can safely run it faster it will reduce my costs materially."

With the addition of the usual salutation and possibly of a request that the information be sent as promptly as possible, this would be the normal and natural letter to write.

But when we start to dictate a letter, all too often something seems to change within us, and we fall back into the use of stereotyped words and phrases.

Here are some we should be especially careful to avoid:

Your letter was duly received. . . .

The word "duly" was probably first used to mean that your letter arrived in the normal and appropriate manner and on time. Since practically all letters are so received, no such explanation is needed unless the letter is *not* "duly" received.

This is to advise you that we have opened . . . .

The word "advise" is wholly unnecessary here. "We have opened, etc." gives the reader all of the information in fewer words. The word "advise" should seldom, if ever, be used in normal business or personal correspondence except in its usual meaning, which is "to recommend a course of action or to counsel." Either "He told me" or "He wrote me about the changes" is much better usage and, also, gives more explicit information than "He advised me of the changes."

We beg to advise . . .

This is even worse. There is no reason why we should need either to beg or to advise.

You will find attached hereto (or enclosed herewith) . . .

The word "hereto" or "herewith" is unnecessary. Also the word "attached" is frequently used in error when added material is enclosed, but *not* attached. Use whichever of these two words is correct.

"You will find" is wholly unnecessary. It is safe to assume that the reader will find the enclosure since you have told him that it is there.

We are in receipt of your kind favor of recent date concerning . . .

"Thank you for your letter of June 5, concerning" gives more information and gives it in a less stilted form.

These are just a few of the stereotyped expressions which are much too frequently used in business correspondence. Any good book on letter writing will give many more.

Some experts in the field of letter writing use and recommend unusual and even spectacular opening sentences, especially in sales letters and in collection letters. These are probably all right for the experts, but for most of us it is better to stick to a simple, tactful, and straightforward statement of our proposition. We will be much less likely to antagonize people.

Simplicity and Clearness

There is an old saying which certainly applies to letters. It is: *Whatever CAN be misunderstood WILL be misunderstood.*

There are few, if any, failures in letter writing which can cause more trouble and ill will than to have in our letters statements which can easily be misunderstood.

Even an out-and-out error can usually be admitted, explained, and settled to the customer's full satisfaction much more easily than can a statement which may easily be taken to mean something different from our intended meaning.

Write simply—short words, short sentences, short paragraphs.

Use short, familiar, everyday words. They are not only easier to understand, but, somehow, they also seem more friendly.

However, in our effort to use simple words, we must be most careful to avoid any appearance of "talking down" to the person to whom we are writing.

For example we should never say, "This is somewhat technical and complicated, but I shall try to explain it in simple, non-technical words so you will have no trouble in understanding it."

We should just describe it in simple, non-technical words, without any introductory comment. This will offend no one.

Of course, in a letter to a person in the same profession or business as the writer, technical or trade terms should be used, since their meaning are usually more precise and restricted than the simpler more general words. And both the writer and recipient understand the exact meaning.

Whether the letter is in simple, non-technical language or in technical language, short sentences and short paragraphs help.

It is especially important that each main topic be given a separate paragraph. This is true, probably especially true, if the topic can be discussed adequately in one sentence. It is so easy to overlook any one sentence buried in a long paragraph.

Correct and Complete in the Information Given

There are few things more exasperating than to have written for some information and to find when you receive the reply that some essential part has been omitted.

And it is easy to do this. For example, Mr. Brown wrote for Bulletin M. Here was the reply:

> Dear Mr. Brown:
>
> We regret very much that our supply of this bulletin in the central office has been completely exhausted.
>
> However, most of our district offices have ample supplies and we are quite sure you will be able to secure a copy from the nearest office to you.
>
> Sincerely yours,

This letter is unsatisfactory in two ways:

First, the writer should not have assumed that Mr. Brown knows the location of the nearest district office. Quite probably he will need to write a second letter, which means added expense and loss of good will.

Second, the letter would have rendered real friend-making service if the last part of the second paragraph had been changed to read:

". . . and we are asking our office at ———— to send you a copy."

A carbon copy of the letter to Mr. Brown, mailed to the district office, would have given that office all of the information it needed. So the added expense would have been negligible.

It is *thinking* to do little things like this which is so important in building good will.

Pleasing in Tone

Think and talk about the reader's wants, the reader's importance. Try to use the words *you* and *yours* much more frequently than *I* and *mine* or even *we* and *ours*.

This would seem to be so simple and so obvious a requirement that it would hardly need to be mentioned, but it is surprising indeed how hard it seems to be to do it even in a "thank-you" letter as, for example, a letter written specifically to thank a customer for having opened a charge account. In the first sentence and just possibly even in the second we would put the emphasis entirely on how important the new customer is to us.

But that is about as long as we can keep from talking about ourselves—our wonderful service, how *we,* all of *us,* are thinking about nothing else but making *our* service and *our* merchandise the best in the world.

It would seem, almost, as if our main objective were to tell the customer how fortunate he should feel to have an account with *us.*

This example is a bit exaggerated, of course, *but not very much.* The next time you open a new account check the "thank-you" letter which comes to you (if you get one at all) to see how little the example really is exaggerated.

Some years ago I had occasion to make a study of the letters to customers from the adjustment department of a large store. Store policy was such that seldom ever was a request refused, no matter how unreasonable.

Many of the letters opened with a rather strong implication that the request was unreasonable, "but because of our famous liberal policy, the request is being granted." In some cases it was almost as if the letter had said:

> Dear Madam:
> I am going to give you everything you asked for in your letter of September 27, but, first, I insist on slapping you in the face.

We should always remember that if we offend even slightly by what we say in our letter or by how we say it we have decreased the effectiveness of the letter as a whole by just that much.

And if we make the reader really angry, then we might much better not have written the letter at all.

On the other hand, if we please the reader by making him feel more important, the effectiveness of every part of the letter is increased.

Our letters will make friends for ourselves and our organizations and create interest in our product only when they show sincere friendliness and interest in the persons to whom they are sent.

Concise

Use enough words to make sure that the purpose of the letter will be accomplished, and no more.

But it should never be forgotten that one of the most important parts of the purpose of *every* letter is to build good will for the organization.

Often it takes only a few additional words to change curtness to courtesy, as illustrated by these two examples:[1]

Curt

> Dear Sir:
>
> Here is the bulletin you asked for. If you want further information, please write us.
>
> Yours very truly,

Courteous

> Dear Mr. Weston:
>
> We are pleased to send you the attached bulletin, which you requested. If we can be of any more help, just let us know.
>
> Sincerely yours,

---

[1] The letters are quoted from Riebel, John P., *How to Write Successful Business Letters in 15 Days* (Englewood Cliffs, N.J.: Prentice-Hall, Inc., 1953, p. 62).

Plan Your Letters in Advance

Careful advance planning is an important help in meeting every requirement of a good letter, especially clearness, completeness, and correctness.

First, make sure that you have all of the required information clearly, correctly, and in all needed detail.

Second, while both this information and the contents of the letter to be answered are still fresh in your mind, prepare a brief written plan for your reply. This may be somewhat like the one shown below, or even more abbreviated. If possible include in the plan some brief pleasing personal comment.

Thanks
Can furnish all parts
We need info
1. ____________
2. ____________
3. ____________
Ship one week after info
Congrat on #67 win

Third, clip the information and plan to the letter to be answered, so it will be immediately available when you are ready to dictate.

Fourth, after the letter has been dictated and transcribed give it a final review with these questions in mind:

1. Is it written simply and naturally—completely free from stereotyped phrases?
2. Is the information so clearly stated that there is practically no possibility of it being misunderstood?
3. Is *all* necessary information included? Is it in logical order and in short paragraphs so that there is no likelihood of something being overlooked?

4. Is the letter pleasing in tone? If practicable, has a pleasing personal comment been included?
5. Are the general appearance, spelling, grammar, etc., up to the desired standard?
6. Will the letter as a whole be effective in accomplishing the desired purpose?

How to Write Effective Reports

The ability to write effective reports can and usually does play a much more important part in how fully success is achieved in the modern business world than is commonly realized.

Even if you have not yet attained as much as junior executive status, you have an opportunity, through the suggestion system, to show your ability to prepare a "report" on some situation which you think can be improved. If your suggestion contains a concise but fully adequate description and analysis of the situation as it is and a clean-cut but definitely tactful recommendation for improvement, it will often gain for you that favorable notice by higher executives so important to success.

If you are a junior executive supervising a small department, there will probably be monthly and possibly annual reports. These can be dull, unorganized listings of routine things done. They can be too boastful in an obvious bid for executive notice. Or they can include all of the needed routine data in a well-organized manner and can also, concisely and tactfully, give added information which may point to some desirable improvements and, possibly, definite recommendations for such improvements.

If you are a senior executive, well-planned and well-executed reports, both from the executives to whom you have delegated responsibility and authority and from you to your chief, are not only helpful to your success, they are absolutely essential.

Three Kinds of Reports

The three kinds of reports which the executive in business will be most frequently called upon to prepare are periodic reports of operations, reports of investigations with recommendations, and merit ratings.

Of these, individual merit ratings are often not considered as "reports" in the same sense that an investigation of some unsatisfactory condition is so considered, but they are most important reports. On the carefulness, completeness, and accuracy of each merit rating often depends whether some employee is given an opportunity for the advancement he deserves.

All of these reports go to higher executives. They are written primarily to give a picture of some situation or condition and to make recommendations. But, much more than the writer may realize, they give to the higher executive a true picture of the writer. Is he thorough? Does he think and write clearly? Is he tactful? Is he intellectually honest?

It would, I believe, be of decided value to our success and to the success of the organizations for which we work if all of us realized more fully how accurately and how clearly the reports we prepare show to others our abilities, our personalities, and even our characters.

Seven Characteristics of a Good Report

A good report *of any kind* should, to the fullest extent possible, be honest, accurate, complete, clear, concise, tactful, and well organized.

Honest. It is obvious that any report which tries to paint a brighter picture of the success of any operation than is justified by facts or one that omits or minimizes facts not favorable to the writer's recommendations, is worse than useless.

Accurate. It is by no means easy to get all of the facts accurately and to present them uncolored by personal bias, but every effort should be made to do so.

Complete. The facts should be stated and conditions described in sufficient detail so that there can be no misconceptions. Of course the knowledge the reader has of the situation and of any technical or trade terms used will have bearing on how detailed the report must be.

Clear. It is usually a good practice, after the report is written in rough draft form, for the writer to read it carefully to see if any statement could possibly be misunderstood. If someone else will read it and tell the writer what *he* thinks it means, that is even better. Often just hearing anything read aloud will cause us to notice imperfections we would never have noticed no matter how many times we might have read it ourselves.

Concise. A report should contain all of the words, illustrations, even stories of what has happened that are needed to make the meaning fully clear to the reader, but no words, no illustrations, no stories which are not needed in the accomplishment of this purpose.

Tactful. Too often we forget that tactfulness is as important in reports as it is in letters. This is especially true in reports which recommend changes in organization or procedure. It is a natural tendency for anyone to defend the way he has been doing anything. And if the recommendation or some other part of the report is tactlessly critical, this tendency is increased tremendously. Here is an example:

Some years ago I was superintendent of a store which was a member of a group of several stores. Each year the superintendents met in one of the stores and, as part of the program, made a thorough study of the service of that store. At one of these meetings we met to listen to part of the report which had been written by one of the superintendents whose shoppers had reported some examples of poor service. When the superintendent came to his rather untactful comment concerning that service, one member of the group interrupted with the comment, "Swell, that'll burn 'em up!"

On the whole, the report was a good one and there were many helpful suggestions. But I doubt if either the president or store superintendent derived one half the good from the report they would have had if it had not "burned 'em up."

Well Organized. The arrangement should be logical. There should be headings and subheadings identifying the various parts so the reader can easily locate any part he wishes to read again.

I worked under a store president some years ago who had these thoroughly worthwhile rules about reports:

1. There must be an identifying title on each report (subject, who wrote it, date, etc.).
2. All reports must be typed double space.
3. As nearly as practicable the facts justifying each recommendation should be placed immediately following the recommendation.
4. If the report is over three pages in length, there must be a summary, especially of recommendations, on the first page, including the numbers of the pages on which the full recommendation and the facts justifying the recommendation are given.

How to Make Written or Oral Suggestions to Higher Executives

"Mr. Grant, I would like to make a suggestion for an organizational change and I am sure, if you had had this plan in operation, things would never have got into the mess they are in now."

"Where did you get the idea that things are in a mess?" replied Mr. Grant. "A few minor changes were necessary and we have already made those. Is that all you wanted to see me about, Mr. Brown?"

Mr. Grant was president of a department store with about a thousand employees and Mr. Brown was an exceptionally bright young junior executive in that store.

I was, at the time, familiar enough with the situation to know that Mr. Brown did have some really excellent suggestions. Also, one department definitely was "in a mess."

Mr. Grant was a capable executive who, as a rule, welcomed suggestions, but I do not believe he ever listened to Mr. Brown's suggestion.

Mr. Brown left the organization several months later to accept a better position and, the last I heard, had won several promotions.

Evidently he had learned, at least, how *not* to make suggestions to a higher executive.

But how *should* a junior executive make a suggestion to a higher executive?

There are no special rules, other than the admonition to be most careful to follow the four rules which actually we should always follow when making a suggestion to anyone. These rules are:

1. *Be tactful throughout.* Be most careful to avoid, especially in the opening, any statement which might be construed as a personal criticism. When the suggestion actually involves a change in how the person himself should do something, it is more tactful to say, "I believe it might get better results *if that were done* in this manner," rather than *"if you would do that,* etc."

2. *Have a clear and logical explanation well prepared.* If we have any vagueness or confusion in our own minds, the person to whom we are talking will certainly not get a clear understand-

ing of what we are suggesting. And if he does not have a clear picture there is little or no chance of the suggestion being accepted.

3. *Have a well-prepared statement of advantages.* The person to whom we are making the suggestion is, and rightfully should be, on the defensive. It costs money and creates confusion to make changes. The executive should not accept suggestions unless the probable results are worth the cost. Some executives make it a rule not to make a change unless the estimated savings are twice the estimated cost. They do this because estimates are so likely to be on the optimistic side, and seldom do they take into account the cost in confusion always caused by any change.

4. *Anticipate and be prepared to meet objections.* The executive would be foolish indeed if he did not consider the objectionable features as well as the advantages of any suggestion offered. Do not consider this as any criticism of you or of your judgment. It is the only sound method of reaching a wise decision. Be prepared to answer any objections calmly, objectively, and tactfully.

Summary

The principal requirements for success in writing letters and reports which will be effective in accomplishing their desired objectives may be summarized in four words, Tactfulness, Clearness, Completeness, Correctness.

Tactfulness. If the letter or report irritates or antagonizes the person to whom it is sent, there is little chance of its securing favorable action no matter how completely it satisfies all of the other requirements.

Clearness. We should keep constantly in mind the old saying, "Whatever *can* be misunderstood *will* be misunderstood." And few things can cause more wasted time than statements which can be misunderstood.

Completeness. There are few things more exasperating to the recipient of a letter or report than to have some essential information omitted.

Correctness of information. Nothing is more inexcusable or can cause more trouble than incorrect information. Check and double check.

It is impossible to discuss adequately in one chapter so important a subject as writing letters and reports. Some further study is recommended.

Three books which have been helpful to me in my work are:

Riebel, John P., *How to Write Successful Business Letters in 15 Days,* Englewood Cliffs, N.J.: Prentice-Hall, Inc., 1953.

Smart, Walter K., Louis W. McElvey, and Richard C. Gerfen, *Business Letters,* New York: Harper & Brothers, Fourth Edition, 1957.

Brown, Leland, *Effective Business Report Writing,* Englewood Cliffs, N.J.: Prentice-Hall, Inc., 1955.

11

HOW TO SPEAK EFFECTIVELY IN PUBLIC AND ENJOY IT

Dear Mr. Clark:

The members of the Executives' Club of Portland have heard from a number of sources about the splendid production record your department has made, and we know that the story of how you have accomplished this will be most interesting to all of us.

We would like very much to have you as principal speaker at our luncheon meeting at the Brown Hotel on Tuesday, October 14, at 1:00 o'clock.

May we count on you?

Sincerely yours,

/s/ John A. Sanders
Chairman—Program Committee

What would be YOUR first reaction if YOU should receive a similar invitation to speak before some group interested in your type of work? Would it be, as it should, a feeling of deep gratification that your efforts had been recognized and an enthusiastic welcome of the opportunity to tell your story to so important a club, or would it be a feeling of fear, almost panic, with a mad scramble to find some plausible excuse why you could not possibly accept the invitation?

With all too many executives, really capable executives, it would be the latter.

Every business executive is called upon from time to time to address some group—a luncheon club, a professional convention, a meeting of his fellow citizens interested in some civic project, his board of directors, or the employees who work under his supervision—and it is becoming increasingly important that he be able to do this well. Few of us are or aspire to be orators; yet it is a definite asset to any executive, or to any person who aspires to be an executive, to be able to capture and hold the attention of a group of people with a simple, sincere, and enthusiastic talk.

Fortunately, if one does not already have this ability, he will not find it difficult to acquire. The rules are few and simple. But some may be tempted to interrupt at this point and ask, as did one executive at a meeting where this subject was being discussed: "I have no doubt, as you say, that the rules are few and simple," he said, "but what good does that do me if I am so paralyzed by fear every time I try to get up to say a few words that I completely forget everything I know? What I want to know first of all is how to overcome fright—and I mean fright, not just nervousness."

That is not too difficult either. We usually dread to make a speech because we fear that we may suddenly forget some important part of what we had planned to say and to find ourselves speechless, or that we may get our sentence structure mixed and say something ludicrous or do something else which will cause us to feel embarrassed in front of our friends. It is comforting to know that even experienced speakers are not entirely immune from this fear, and that they often protect themselves from the possibility of having just such embarrassing situations occur by using certain simple devices or "tricks of the trade." It is also comforting to know that the person who speaks in public only occasionally may, to a large degree, remove the possibility of the occurrences he dreads by the use of these same "tricks." And with the cause of fear removed, fear itself largely vanishes.

So let us assume that you are Mr. Clark and that you decided to accept the invitation.

Let us assume, also, that you do not speak in public often and that you have accepted with some fear and trembling. If we are wrong in this assumption and you are an experienced speaker you will not need the suggestions which follow, because you will have built up your own technique.

But if we are right and you do feel the need for all the help and advice you can get, then I believe firmly that careful and conscientious following of the 17 practical rules of public speaking which follow will enable you to make a talk of which you need not be ashamed. Included in these rules are what we have called "tricks of the trade," the devices which many experienced speakers use to help them banish fear.

Seventeen Practical Rules for Success in Public Speaking

1. Choose your exact subject with care.

First, choose your general subject in a field with which you are thoroughly familiar. It gives a sense of security when you are confident that your knowledge is broad enough so that, should you forget some little point you had planned to use, you have more material readily available. Also, there is comfort in the knowledge that, should someone in the audience ask a practical or even a technical question, you can probably answer it.

The general subject decided upon, the next question is: "In

what part of this general subject will this particular group be most interested?" Persons in different occupations are interested in different phases of any one subject. For example, if you were an employment manager and were giving a talk on "The Central Employment Office" you would probably stress the different phases of the subject for different groups in about this manner:

Accountants: Cost saving and prevention of payroll "padding."

General Executives: Savings of executive time in interviewing and service to department heads needing help.

Preachers: Social services to be rendered through helping people to find the right jobs.

Personnel Executives: Description and evaluation of forms and methods used.

In what phase of *your* work is *your* audience interested?

Do not accept an impossible subject. An engineering professor was asked to talk to a joint meeting of county commissioners and highway engineers on, "The Design of the Small Highway Bridge." Realizing that the county commissioners were, for the most part, business men or farmers rather than engineers, he spent the first 15 minutes of his time in explaining the meaning of such technical terms as "bending moment," "factor of safety," "shear," etc. This was, to say the least, boring to his engineer listeners, and, since it is practically impossible to explain these terms adequately in 15 minutes, it was equally boring to the county commissioners. The result was that no one either enjoyed his talk or profited from it.

Had he changed his subject to "Modern Traffic and the Small Highway Bridge," and told of the changes modern traffic has made necessary in the design and cost of small bridges, he would probably have interested both groups. And the program committee would, undoubtedly, have been quite willing to accept the change.

It is well to remember that when the program chairman mentions a subject in his invitation, he does not mean that the exact subject must be used. He is almost always willing to accept suggestions from you as to a change which will give the group something of greater interest.

2. *Write just as the ideas occur to you.*

After you have selected carefully your exact subject, start to write. Write rapidly, whatever you think will be interesting. Do not give too much thought to order, sentence structure, choice of the exact word or the absolute accuracy of statistical data. Ideas are what you are interested in now, and if you stop to think about which of two words expresses better your exact meaning, you will lose your inspiration. Write both words and make the necessary corrections later. Write about only one topic on each sheet of paper so that later you can conveniently arrange your material in the most effective order. Write more than you plan to use.

In your writing and in your talk *use the simple narrative form as much as is possible.* Not only is this form by far the easiest to use, it is, also, the most interesting to an audience and the most effective both in teaching and in moving a group to action.

And it can be used effectively even in the presentation of abstract facts and theories. Perhaps the reason so many of us remember something about Newton's Law and have forgotten almost everything else we learned about physics is that, for the most of us, our first acquaintance with this law came through the story of how one day when the great scientist was resting under a tree, an apple fell and hit him on the head, and how that occurrence started him to thinking on the question of why the apple fell toward him rather than he toward the apple. Almost every rule or principle can be explained more easily and more effectively by the use of some illustration of its application than by an abstract discussion.

One other advantage of the narrative form of presentation is that it makes unnecessary the memorizing of an outline. You can usually remember the order in which to present the various parts of a narrative, but you might find it difficult to remember the order in which you had planned to present the parts of any other type of talk.

3. Do not hesitate to use the first person.

Today, more than ever before, experienced speakers are using the first person in everything but formal technical papers.

A description of the cities and peoples of one of the countries which is in the headlines is made even more interesting if the speaker can say: "The peculiar attitude of the people of that country toward foreigners can probably best be explained by telling the story of what happened to one member of our party, etc."

This combines the use of the first person and the narrative form. Do this whenever you can.

Also, it is often much less antagonizing to say, "We believe the best way to solve that problem is . . . . , because, etc.", than it is to say "The best way to solve that problem is . . . . , because, etc." And the less antagonizing your statements are, the more likely they are to win people to your way of thinking.

People, all of us, are like children. If anyone antagonizes us, whatever he may say later, no matter how reasonable, is almost completely ineffective.

But there are pitfalls in the use of the first person which should be most carefully avoided.

It must always be remembered that *what any audience enjoys most is having its ego raised.* The speaker whose use of the first person carries with it any semblance of bragging soon becomes unpopular. Occasional reference to how you have succeeded is all right, but with it there should be some stories of the times you failed. Jack Benny's great popularity is due largely to the fact that he has the good sense to let us laugh at him, and we enjoy that. *Tell a few jokes on yourself.*

4. Plan your opening sentences with especial care.

Your opening sentences should accomplish three things: (1) win the good will of your audience, (2) arouse interest, and (3) lead that interest naturally into your presentation of your subject.

Look over what you have written and decide which of all the ideas will make the most interesting opening.

What is said during the first 30 seconds is of great importance in any speech; the shorter the speech the more important. A successful speaker to business groups once told me that he often spent at least a third of his time of preparation in deciding just what should be his opening sentence or two, a third in planning his closing sentences, and the remaining third on all the rest of his talk.

It is usually a good practice virtually to memorize the opening sentences. Each word has been carefully chosen and should be given exactly as planned.

Then, too, most of us who do not speak often are especially nervous during the first few seconds after we stand up. If we can make a good start, this helps a great deal to dispel the feeling. *The remainder of the talk should seldom, if ever, be memorized.*

The first objective of any speaker is to gain the good will of his audience, to get them to like him. This is done best by making some complimentary statement about them.

But this statement should, if possible, be tied into the subject rather than to use the frequent, "I want first to say how happy I am to be here, etc." One woman executive accomplished this in a talk to a group of businessmen by saying:

"I always like to speak to a group of men because I believe men think more logically than women do and are not so often swayed by emotional prejudices. And the subject I want to discuss with you tonight needs just such intelligent consideration" (15 seconds).

A somewhat similar beginning which accomplishes both the first and second step of the opening was used with pleasing effect in a talk on "Training for Leadership," made to a group of preachers:

"For anyone to attempt to talk to this group on the subject of Leadership is like 'bringing coals to Newcastle.' No one can live in Columbia long and fail to realize how great an influence for good on the lives of all of the people of this community is exercised by the churches of Columbia. And the reason is unquestionably the splendid leadership of the men here in this room. But I have always found that those who know the most about any subject are always the most eager to learn more—so here I am with my little wagon of coals" (33 seconds).

Many teachers of public speaking recommend the use of a much more dramatic opening. This is all right for the experienced speaker, but for the rest of us it is probably better to start with a simple opening in which there are no difficult words, and certainly no attempt to be highly dramatic from almost the first word.

Personally, I always prefer to start with something like: "I wonder how many of you remember—" or "It was just three years ago this week that many of us here tonight—" or "A few weeks ago, in a store in New York I had an unpleasant experience which made me ask myself the question, 'Could that have happened in our store?'—etc."

These openings lead easily into dramatic statements, but they give me an opportunity to get control of my voice before it is necessary for me to say anything dramatic. I strongly advise anyone who, like myself, is somewhat nervous at the start of his talk to use this method.

It is wise also to plan even what you will say in thanking the chairman for his introduction. Make it brief and simple.

"Thank you, Mr. Chairman, for that somewhat too flattering introduction" is usually appropriate. Introductions are almost always flattering. If not, it is easy to cut your comment down to, "Thank you, Mr. Chairman."

A humorous story makes an excellent opening, provided it leads naturally into the subject of the talk and provided, also, it is well told. But a story, no matter how good or how well told, which has no relation to the subject is likely to divert interest from your subject.

5. *Prepare your closing sentences with as much thought and care as you did your opening sentences.*

The objective is to have your audience take away from the meeting a feeling of good will toward you and your cause, a clear understanding of and agreement with the conclusions you reached, and a definite determination to do the things which your talk has advocated.

This ending will usually take the form of a brief summary of the principal conclusions and a forceful, but always tactful, appeal to take some action, either individually or in a group.

The less stiff and formal this summary is, the better. There are occasions when the speaker should say, "In conclusion I should like to sum up, etc." but, as a rule it is much better to approach the summary less formally.

6. Arrange the balance of your talk in logical order; then review the entire talk.

Your talk should lead naturally, step by step, from your opening sentences to your planned conclusion.

After you have done this, read carefully what you have written and challenge each sentence with these questions:

a. Is it necessary; does it contribute anything worthwhile?

b. Is it tactful; can it give offense to any one?

c. Am I, by any chance, indulging in a little bragging?

d. Is the sentence clear in its meaning, free from errors in grammar or needless words.

e. Is it easy and natural for me to use the words which I have written? Read the talk aloud and if it does not read easily, change it so that it will.

7. Choose a title for your talk which is interesting and appealing.

A title which is both a true designation of what you will actually talk about and, also, arouses the curiosity is often better than a more prosaic title.

"The WHY of Human Behavior" or "People Want only Five Things" would probably be more appealing to a group of businessmen than "Psychological Aspects of Human Behavior."

"The Science of Retailing in Forty-Five Words" might bring a few more members of the Merchant's Association to a meeting than "Fundamental Principles of Retailing."

But unusual titles like these will backfire and take away from the effectiveness of your talk unless you can deliver. If, when you begin to talk, you present only some farfetched connection between your curiosity-arousing title and what you say, you may have the unpleasant experience of seeing interest go down the way a toy balloon does when someone lets the air out of it.

We should always remember that curiosity-arousing subjects should be used only when we are sure we can deliver.

8. Plan Visual Aids.

Whether or not it is wise to use visual aids depends largely on whether the talk is essentially inspirational or essentially informational. In the inspirational talk it is usually not wise because, primarily, you want your audience to *feel* strongly about some cause, and anything which requires the audience to look for a time at the blackboard or chart and then at you has a tendency to take away from the emotional appeal of your talk. One exception is where a motion picture is shown which presents some condition which needs correction, such as overcrowded schools or unsanitary conditions in a slum area, and this is followed by an appeal to the group to do its part in remedying that condition. In this case the visual aid builds up the proper emotional condition for the talk, but does not interrupt the talk.

In talks of an informational character, however, visual aids, properly planned and used, are of great value.

A portable blackboard on which to write the main points as they are developed or charts prepared in advance for the same purpose are the aids most frequently used.

If charts are used, they should be "flip charts," so as to have only one point at a time appear. If all of the points which you plan to make are on the first chart the audience will feel that it already knows what you plan to talk about and will not feel the need to listen to your talk.

There is something a little less cut and dried about points written on the blackboard as you speak than about the same points on a chart which obviously was prepared before the meeting and in which the audience cannot possibly have had any part.

If your points are to be put on the board as developed, it is desirable to arrange with someone to do the writing as you direct so as to avoid the necessity of your turning your back to the audience even for a short time. Go over the points in advance with this person and have some signal planned so that he will know just when to write. He should sit—not stand—near the board and arise as needed. Rarely, if ever, should the speaker do his own writing, as he loses touch with the audience and wastes time.

Occasionally speakers hand out photographs or other material to be looked at and passed on to the next person. This is a poor practice, since it practically asks the listeners to cease being listeners.

9. Decide carefully whether or not to read your talk.

There is no exact formula. The answer depends on two things, the nature of the talk and your own ability and freedom from nervousness.

A technical paper or any long and somewhat involved discussion of any subject should, undoubtedly, be read. Even a 15- to 20-minute talk is more interesting when well read than if the speaker is likely to forget one or two of his more important points and then try to go back to them.

Reading the talk eliminates this possibility, and the talk will be made much more interesting if the following suggestions are followed:

a. Have the talk typed *triple* space with wide margins.

b. Practice reading it aloud while you are standing.

c. Underscore with red pencil words you want to emphasize, mark places where you will wish to pause, and make any other marks which will help.

d. Get familiar enough with the talk so that parts, especially narratives, can be given without looking at the paper.

e. Arrange to have available some kind of a lectern. A talk appears to be much more informal when you have your copy on the lectern and you can occasionally step to one side and talk informally for a few moments without holding your paper in your hand. And there is one other advantage for speakers, like you and me, who are somewhat nervous. The lectern gives us something to hold on to. And, if our hands shake a little, no one sees it.

f. Have your copy in a three-ring notebook with rings just large enough for the pages to turn easily.

All of these things help to make a talk which is read as interesting as is possible, but, if you can give your talk without reading it, it will be even more interesting.

You will find, too, as you look into the faces of the people in your audience, that they will give something back to you. You will see in which parts your audience is most interested, and you can expand a little there and contract somewhere else. You will now be talking *with* the people in your audience instead of *at* them. Both you and the audience will enjoy it much more.

10. Now, some "tricks of the trade."

Have full notes in your pocket. My own greatest fear has always been that my mind may go blank, especially early in the talk. So I always have reasonably complete notes on a few cards which I can carry quite unobtrusively in my hand. And on the first card I usually have the complete first sentence or two. Seldom if ever do I need to look at the cards for the opening, but it is a comfort to know that I *can* do so.

Now here is one more thing I often do which you surely will laugh at, and I don't blame you. In addition to the cards I usually have in my pocket much fuller notes, sometimes the entire talk.

And here is how this practice started.

I was teaching a night-school class in personnel management and had been fortunate enough to have the State Labor Commissioner consent to speak to the group. I had just about reached the middle of my introduction when suddenly I realized that the Commissioner's name had completely left my memory. I was about to panic until I remembered that I had in my pocket a typed list of the offices he had held and a description of his other accomplishments.

So I remarked that "our speaker has had so many high honors that I fear I may omit some if I do not read the list." Of course, his name was on the list. A real disaster was averted.

And so now I seldom talk to any group without having at least rather full notes in my pocket. I have never yet needed to refer to these notes, but what a comfort it is to know that they are there.

I do not know how many really experienced speakers do this same thing, but I suspect that many of them do.

Be at the meeting place ahead of time; check to see that every detail has been taken care of. Few things can add more to any nervousness you may feel about speaking than to leave home so late that you have only barely time enough to get to the meeting place and then, as your car waits at a stop light, to wonder if your chart rack has been set up and other details taken care of.

It is an excellent practice to get to the meeting place in time to check everything and still have about 15 minutes to sit quietly and review what you are going to say. This will build up in your mind a feeling of confidence and of enthusiasm for your subject.

Eat lightly; avoid carbonated drinks. Eat lightly before you speak. If one eats at all heavily when he is nervous, gas is likely to be formed in the stomach and that is embarrassing to say the least.

And do not make the mistake I once made of taking a carbonated drink during the intermission just before my time to speak. You can imagine the result, and the embarrassment it caused.

Do not apologize. When you are introduced, rise, turn to the chairman and acknowledge the introduction, then turn to your audience and pause for just a second or two before you begin your prepared opening. Most inexperienced speakers start too quickly. The audience is looking at the chairman as he introduces you; give it time to transfer its attention to you.

And if there is any one rule to be remembered above all others by the inexperienced speaker it is, *do not apologize!* Nothing weakens a talk more than an explanation at the start that the speaker is unaccustomed to speaking in public and that he hopes the audience will bear with him. If your talk is poor, your audience will know it without your saying so, but the chances are that it will not be poor. You know your subject; you have made careful preparation; you believe sincerely in what you plan to say; you have every requisite for making a good talk.

The chances are all in your favor. Why spoil your chances by beginning with an apology?

Do not try to "ad-lib" at the beginning of your talk. As a rule it is unwise to depart at all from your planned acknowledgment of the introduction and your planned opening sentences.

As I look back at the times I have tried at the beginning of a talk to "ad-lib" with some "clever" remark which had just occurred to me, I am sure that at least three times out of four the net effect was bad rather than good.

Avoid "Traps." James Williams is, normally, an excellent speaker, but one day he fell into a "trap" which he had unconsciously set for himself. Here is the trap:

"There are at least five good reasons why I believe it to be important that we do this."

He told reason one and reason two skillfully; but suddenly he realized that he could only remember four of the five reasons which he had intended to present, and the harder he tried the more panic-stricken he became. The floundering around which ensued so embarrassed him that the balance of his talk was far below his usual standard.

Be careful not to let yourself into such a trap. Say rather: "There are several good reasons why I believe it to be important that we do this."

Many speakers fear the word "statistics." For them it is a "trap." I always avoided the word until I hit upon the device of saying stāy-tistics, slowly at first and then more rapidly. When spoken rapidly in this way scarcely anyone will notice the difference from the normal pronunciation, and the device keeps this word from being a trap.

Similarly, a way can be found to pronounce other difficult words. Practice pronouncing the words which give you trouble.

11. Dress neatly, simply, comfortably.

The goal to be achieved is to be so simply and neatly dressed that neither you nor any one in the audience thinks anything about your clothes. Avoid unusual jewelry or ornaments of any kind, since anything like that distracts attention.

If it is to be an evening meeting, find out whether or not it is to be formal, and just how formal. There are few things more disconcerting than to be the only one wearing a business suit or, possibly even worse, to be the only one wearing a dinner jacket.

12. Use gestures naturally.

Today most teachers of public speaking advise the student to forget gestures. Be enthusiastic about your subject and you will, just naturally, use the same gestures you do in ordinary conversation, and that is the goal to be achieved.

It is well, however, to try to overcome any little disconcerting habits you may have formed, such as twirling a key chain. Ask some good friend if you do have any such habits and, if so, correct them.

But as to gestures, let your own enthusiasm take care of them.

13. Do not speak to some one person too much.

Often a speaker to a business group makes the mistake of addressing his remarks too much to some one person in the group, usually some important executive who is attending the meeting. This should be carefully avoided. It is embarrassing to the executive in question and gives the other members of the group a feeling that the speaker considers them to be somewhat inferior, and this feeling will quickly kill interest.

14. Encourage discussion from the group.

Often you will want to have discussion from the group after you have completed the main part of your talk. This is especially true if you are describing some condition which you believe needs correction and you want comment and suggestions as to how best to go about making that correction.

And it is usually desirable to get suggestions from the group even if you have some definite plan in mind and even if you are talking to your own employees and therefore have authority to *order* that your plan be carried out. This is true for two very good reasons:

First, discussion will often bring out suggestions of a plan which you will recognize as being better than the one you had in mind.

And, second, you will always have more intelligent and more enthusiastic cooperation if those you are counting on to help you have had a part in making the plan. This is true, and I believe it is correct to say it is especially true, if they are people under your supervision.

An effort should be made to get as many as possible of the members of the group to take part in the discussion.

Perhaps the most important single rule to be followed in order to accomplish this is to make such a comment as, "Thank you, that's fine," or "That is an excellent thought, Mr. Jones," immediately after the first contribution from any member of the group. And you can say this sincerely and enthusiastically no matter how weak and halting that contribution may be, because you need this first contribution more than you need anything else. Without it your meeting may easily be a failure.

If you speak encouragingly, even flatteringly to this first contributor, you will find that others do not hesitate to venture their opinions. But the discussion leader I once heard make the mistake of saying, "No, that's wrong; I am afraid you misunderstood my question," found it most difficult to get things started again.

Even after the discussion is well under way the leader should rarely, if ever, contradict or even criticize a statement made by a member of the group. If it is incorrect the leader can ask for the opinion of the group and someone in the group will correct it. Criticism from the leader would tend to reduce participation.

If someone throws into the discussion a thought which is not on the subject being discussed, some such answer as this may be used: "Thank you, Mr. Brown, that is an interesting suggestion, but we had better confine our discussion for the present to this one phase of the question. We shall not forget your suggestion, however, and if there is time we shall get to it a little later."

The person who is too shy to volunteer an opinion can usually be encouraged to take part by a direct question addressed to him. But make it an easy question, one he is sure to answer well. Often asking him to repeat some interesting comment which he made to you in private is an excellent way to encourage the shy person to take part. Be sure to thank him for the comment.

There are many other devices which the leader may use to provoke the thought necessary to good discussion. Some of these are: general or direct questions by the leader, questions assigned in advance, or the making of a statement by the leader which is not correct, then asking, "Is that true?"

> In answering discussion from the floor, it is always important to take a man at what he meant or would like to have said, rather than at what he actually said. Practical men are often timid about talking publicly. Frequently in the embarrassment of speaking from the floor they say things in a way that if taken literally are quite different from what they intended.
>
> If the leader differs with what they literally said when it is not what they meant, and publicly proves that what they said was wrong, they feel that they have been unfairly treated and say to themselves, "If that's the way the discussion is going to be run, I'll shut up."
>
> If, on the other hand, the leader catches and adequately states the idea that a man was feeling his way toward, but was not able clearly to express, it gives the man a sense of elation and renewed self-confidence.[1]

One danger in the discussion method. One danger in any method which invites free discussion is that some one point of little importance may start a discussion which will take more time than that point justifies. To avoid this, you must always keep control and tactfully move the discussion along so that approximately the correct amount of time is given to each point.

15. Have your watch or a clock where you can see it and CLOSE ON TIME.

It is often difficult to close on time, especially when the preliminaries have taken longer than was planned. Sometimes it may mean a quick revision of what you had planned to say, leaving

---

[1] E. D. Smith, *Psychology for Executives* (New York, Harper & Brothers, 1934).

out some of the less important parts. But whatever it takes to do it, close on time.

16. Practice speaking correctly in everyday conversation.

One reason, perhaps the principal reason, why so many of us find it difficult to speak naturally when we stand before a group is because we have grown so careless in our everyday conversations—careless of sentence structure and grammar, careless in our choice of words, careless in our enunciation. When we do stand before a group and wish to speak correctly, we find it difficult to do so and especially difficult to achieve that naturalness of manner so necessary for success. One executive, who found that careless habits of speech into which he had fallen were embarrassing when he spoke in public, offered to give his young son one cent for each mistake he detected in his father's grammar. It was rather expensive for a time, but it was worth the price!

Also, practice "tongue twisters." Learn to read them rapidly without mistakes. Here is one good one:

"The seething sea ceaseth and it sufficeth me."

Any good book on public speaking will have in it passages especially selected as suitable for this practice. There will also be suggestions, as to enunciation, pronunciation, and methods of improving the voice.

17. Practice speaking in public.

Make, rather than avoid, opportunities to speak in public. The more nervous you are about speaking, the more important this is.

Start by speaking quite informally in small groups such as P.T.A. meetings or church or lodge groups. In many such meetings you do not even need to stand while speaking.

But for the practice to be of the greatest value, gather in advance, all of the information you can about the subject to be discussed and have some facts to back any opinion you may express.

If opportunity offers, enroll in a class in public speaking. Here you will be with a group where everyone is as interested as you are in improving his ability to speak in public and, probably, is fully as nervous about it all.

You will never regret the time, the effort, and the sheer determination it takes to follow these simple rules conscientiously and persistently, because few of the accomplishments any person may have can contribute more both to his success on the job and to the general satisfaction he gets from life than does the ability to capture and hold the attention of a group of people with a simple, sincere, and enthusiastic talk.

And that ability can be acquired!

How to Make Meetings of Your Employees More Interesting

Any meeting can be made interesting. This is especially true of a meeting of your employees, since the information you will present usually has to do directly with things which will contribute to their success in the organization.

Preparation for the meeting. First, before any material is assembled, there should be a clear and definite answer to the question, *What do I want to accomplish by this meeting?* The answer to this should be quite specific. As a rule it will be in terms of something you want your employees to do. You want shop employees always to wear goggles when grinding tools; you want salespeople to be able to help their customers better with problems in home decoration; you want stenographers to be more careful about spelling, punctuation, and grammar.

Consider your listener's wants. You will remember from the discussion in Chapter 5 that the best way to get your listeners to do what you want them to do is to relate your want to something your listeners want and to show how doing what you want done will get for them what they want.

Will it make their work simpler or more pleasant? Will it help them to avoid embarrassing errors? Will it help them to earn more money? Will it give them added security? If it will do any of these or any similar things, that fact should be worked into the meeting plans.

Plan for variety. Have your people come to your meetings with a feeling of expectancy and curiosity.

In the shop there can be an actual demonstration of the operation of a new machine for one meeting. At another meeting all of the work spoiled during the month may be piled on a table and the group asked to guess the cost. In the store, there can be a debate between two pieces of merchandise as to which can do the most for the customer (two salespeople representing the merchandise), or a "spelling bee" type of contest in which salespeople are divided into two groups to see which half has learned best the new fashion facts.

Location. The place where the meeting is held should be such that any passing through the meeting space will be behind the group. The light should be on the speaker rather than shining in the faces of the listeners. These and other "little" things play an important part in the success of the meeting.

Discussion, Questions, Suggestions. All of the recommendations given earlier in the chapter on how best to encourage discussion in a general meeting are at least as important to success in meetings of your employees. Give your listeners as full a part as possible in the making of your plans. Having a real part in the planning makes anyone feel important and enthusiastic about helping to carry out the plan. And this is especially true of rank-and-file employees, because so often they are not given any part other than to carry out orders.

Follow-up. The follow-up after the meeting to see that the teaching has carried over into actual practice is as important as actual teaching. Persistent but tactful follow-up is necessary if the teaching is to form permanent habits of action, and that is the real measure of the success of your meetings.

SELF RATING ON PUBLIC SPEAKING

Using the same system you have used in the preceding chapters, rate yourself on these two questions.

Taking into account exactly how important it is to you in a business way, and the personal satisfaction the ability would give you, how adequate to your needs do you consider your present ability in *Public Speaking* and *Holding Meetings of Your Employees?* ______

How high do you rate your actual present efforts to improve this ability when you compare it with what you believe you could and should be doing? ______

12

HOW TO PLAN FOR HAPPY YEARS AFTER RETIREMENT

IT IS QUITE POSSIBLE THAT SOME MAY THINK THAT this chapter does not apply to them. It may be 15 or even more years before they will retire. Why then should they bother about retirement now?

But it does apply to them, perhaps even more than to those for whom retirement is only a year or two away.

This is true because, more often than not, it is only through long and careful planning that the years after retirement can be made to be truly happy years.

But any planning, no matter how short a time there is, is better than no planning at all. So, whether you have one month or 20 years to prepare for retirement, it is my earnest advice that you read carefully the suggestions which follow and put as many of them into practice as possible. Whatever effort this may take, including even some skimping financially, is thoroughly worth the price.

I know this to be true not only because I have seen it work out that way in the experience of others, but also because it has worked so well in my own case.

I retired a little over four years ago after having followed carefully every suggestion I am recommending that others follow. And I believe that these four years have been, for my wife and me, the happiest years of our lives.

I am doing, on a half-time basis, the one type of work I enjoy doing more than any other; we have more time to do things together than we have ever had before; and finally, although there is no large income, there is enough to do many of the not-too-expensive things we had always wanted to do, but could never before find time to do. *What more could anyone want!*

Here was my plan and I believe, with some changes to adjust it to special circumstances, it will work for anyone.

About 18 years before the date of my mandatory retirement, I arranged to have ten percent of my salary diverted into payment for an annuity in addition to that regularly provided.

Some years later, I began to check into possibilities for interesting work for retired men with my training and experience. Several personnel directors of my acquaintance had gone into college teaching when they retired. I had taught for one year immediately after my own graduation and had enjoyed the work very much. So this seemed to be a good field, at least to explore.

Writing is another type of work I enjoy and, during the last ten or twelve years of active work as a personnel director, I wrote several books on various phases of personnel management. Of course I was careful to see that the deans of the two schools of business administration in which I was interested received complimentary copies.

A few years after I reached the age permitting optional retirement, I began to make contacts and before too long, I received my present appointment as Lecturer in Management (part time) in the University of South Carolina.

Mandatory retirement for college teachers is usually at a considerably more advanced age than for most other occupations, but that time will come, so we are "planning" again. And I believe we shall be fully as happy after my second retirement as we are now, possibly even happier.

Altogether too many people, however, still look forward with dread to retirement. Their fear is that they will just lapse into idleness and boredom, and soon wither away and die.

And we cannot blame them too much for believing that retirement is almost a death sentence, since so many people have said so.

Fortunately, they are wrong. Actually, according to insurance tables, older people who have retired do, on the average, live longer than those who stay on the job past the usual retirement age.

Instead of dreading old age, we should look forward to it as offering real possibilities for making the years, especially those after retirement, the happiest years of our lives.

But to realize these possibilities to their fullest extent will require advance planning and preparation, always remembering, as Dr. Harry Emerson Fosdick so aptly puts it in an article in the November, 1959, issue of *Guideposts,* "The secret of a happy retirement is not only to retire *from* something, but to retire *to* something."

Goals

Any planning is more effective in achieving the desired over-all result if definite goals are set.

For peace of mind and happiness in full measure the retired person needs as nearly as is possible all of the six things listed below, and all advance planning and preparation should be with these six needs as definite goals to be striven for:

1. Some regular work which is interesting, pride-building, not too "high pressure," and, usually, bringing in some pay.
2. Reasonable financial security and freedom from worry.

3. A feeling of independence, "standing on his own two feet."

4. Pleasant companionship—some old people, but not all old people.

5. As nearly perfect health as medical care and his own co-operation with the doctor can give him.

6. But the greatest need of all of us, both old and young, is for appreciation and love. And as we grow older this need grows stronger and stronger.

Each of these goals will be discussed separately.

A Suitable Occupation

An occupation to be considered fully suitable to the needs of the retired person should meet all of the following requirements:

1. The person should enjoy doing the work involved.
2. The occupation should be reasonably "pride-building."
3. There should be as little "high pressure" as possible.
4. It should allow more leisure time than did the pre-retirement occupation.
5. It should not involve any serious risk of losing too great a part of whatever financial reserve there may be.

Enjoying the work. It is surprising how many people have satisfactorily solved the problem of selecting a suitable occupation by first deciding what two or three things they liked to do best (including hobbies and avocations) and then finding someone who would pay them for doing one or more of these things.

This may seem to be an oversimplification of the problem and, of course, it will not work in every case, but it has in a great many cases.

One friend of mine enjoyed electrifying old-fashioned lamps as a hobby. When it became necessary for him to retire, he bought a number of old lamps, often with parts missing. He then wired the better ones for electricity, using some of the lamps which were in the worst condition to furnish parts to complete the others. He has made this a profitable business.

Another turned the hobby of woodworking into a profitable business, making and selling unusual bird houses and other novelties.

And almost every city has a "Fix-it" shop, often owned and operated by a retired man who did this work free of charge for his neighbors before he retired.

The list of work enjoyed most should include, also, regular business occupations. And it should certainly include the part of the person's present work he likes the best.

To help in this, it might be well to review lists of suitable occupations given in books such as may be found in any public library.

This done, there would probably be a list of four or five occupations any one of which would provide enjoyable work.

The next step should be to check each of these occupations against the remaining requirements which an occupation must satisfy to be considered as fully satisfactory. This can be done best by asking questions concerning each occupation under consideration and answering these as they apply to the person's own case.

Is it reasonably "pride-building"? Does it render a worthwhile service to people? Is it something you can do well enough so that you will be proud of your work? It certainly need not be a so-called important occupation. In fact it probably should not be, since such occupations are usually in the "high pressure" category. But it should be one about which your children will not be ashamed to say, "Dad is doing . . . . . and is having the time of his life."

Does it allow at least a little more leisure time than did the job from which you will be retiring? Can you go fishing or hunting or play golf a little more frequently, and in a more relaxed frame of mind?

If it is some type of business for yourself (and this is usually desirable, if practicable), *does it require risking only a relatively small part of your financial reserve?* And, even then, is the risk not so great as to cause worry on your part?

Is it reasonably free from "high pressure"? Must quotas or deadlines be met almost regardless of how you feel? Is there constant fear of something happening which might cause unpleasant consequences for you?

After applying these tests to the occupations being considered, it is highly desirable, if it is at all possible, to try out on a small scale, even before retirement, the one or two of the occupations which have made the best showing. This is especially true (and also somewhat easier to do) if the occupation chosen is some form of business for yourself.

For example, it would neither be difficult nor would it interfere with your regular work if you were to buy a few old lamps, wire them for electricity, and see if you could sell them.

Similarly, you could raise a few fine tomatoes or flowers in your back yard. A neighborhood store would probably be glad to sell them for you without charging too much commission.

Or, if your regular work has been in the accounting field, you might arrange to set up and maintain a bookkeeping system for one or two small businesses.

Teaching in night school is still another "try-out" occupation which will not interfere with your regular work.

Some experience in one or more occupations of this type will help you to find out what work you like well enough to put more time into it after retirement. And it will help you to approach retirement with a greater feeling of confidence.

Finally, however, it always pays to be on the alert and ready to change plans if some unusual opportunity arises as, quite often, it will. But, of course, no one should abandon his carefully thought-out plans without a thorough investigation of the new opportunity.

Reasonable Financial Security

Social security payments have quite largely removed the fear of stark poverty from the minds of those approaching retirement, but that is about all they have done. Even when these payments are supplemented by employer's retirement plans, only little more than necessities are usually provided for.

And probably this is as it should be. If we want a few of the extras which add so much to our comfort and happiness (and we all do want these), we should be willing to do something ourselves to provide for them. This is not too difficult, if we start soon enough to save systematically.

Here is a suggested program:

1. As soon as you can possibly do so, even if it calls for some skimping, start making regular deposits to be used to increase your annuity. Many retirement plans include provision for the purchase of added annuity at lower cost than would be possible if it were purchased individually from an insurance company. Check to see if your company's plan does have this provision.

2. If you are buying your home, plan your payments so that you will own it free and clear before your retirement date.

3. Try, also, to have your automobile and all major household appliances completely paid for.

4. Do not buy speculative stocks unless you definitely can afford to lose.

5. Some plans of group insurance covering hospital and surgical costs allow individual and family coverage to be continued after retirement with no increase in cost. If at all possible, some such arrangement should be made.

6. For practically everyone, however, the total income after retirement will be less than before retirement. The amount of the reduction will, of course, be minimized by having completed payments on the home, automobile, and major appliances, but, as a

rule, some adjustment will be necessary. Decide well in advance what must be given up to adjust comfortably to the reduced income and begin to make the necessary changes at least a year or two before retirement. Your friends will not think any less of you if you do make these changes quite openly and frankly. In fact, anyone worth having as a friend will respect you more if you do.

Independence

As we grow older, most of us long for a time when we can be free from dictation by anyone. With many of us there have been times when, in order to keep our jobs and provide for our families, we have had to work under people whose methods of supervision were, to say the least, not pleasant.

After retirement we long for a greater degree of independence than has been possible before.

We love our children and we want them to love us, but we do not want to live with them, because, if we do, we know that neither they nor we can live the normal, natural lives which they and we desire.

Probably the happiest solution is to live near enough so that each can visit the other often, but not near enough so that *either* will be tempted to try to monopolize the other's time or to run the other's affairs.

However, if this involves moving to a distant city, at least two important conditions must be given careful consideration:

First, the climate of the new location may not be conducive to the health and comfort of older people.

Also, the "children" near to whose home we have moved at considerable expense may, for business reasons, find it to their advantage to move to some other part of the country. If they make the move, we would be left "stranded" in a location chosen only because it was near to them. If they do not make the move we would feel, regardless of assurances to the contrary, that we had caused them to remain against their best interests.

Our determination not to live with our children may even mean living in a home for old people. Here we will, at least, not feel that we are inconveniencing anyone and may find many opportunities for service to others less fortunate than we are. In this way that feeling of being wanted and needed, so important to the happiness of everyone, can be ours.

And, as a rule, we need not be living "on charity." Most homes supported by churches or fraternal organizations are happy to have anyone pay part or all of the cost.

However, homes of this type will seldom accept people who have become bedridden, but will take care of those who become bedridden after they enter. So from every viewpoint, if we plan definitely to live in a home for old people, it is well to make arrangements and to move into the home of our choice while both husband and wife are still reasonably active.

But, wherever we live, there is one important caution we should observe in all of our efforts to achieve independence.

The line between independence and obstinacy is a fine one. And as we grow older, even before we retire, we are sometimes likely to resent well-intentioned advice. Sometimes we refuse to accept suggestions from younger people, especially from our children, even when we had previously practically decided to do the thing suggested.

As one retired person, speaking of his children, expressed it to me, "It is very hard to have somebody tell you what to do even if he does mean well." And it is quite probable that our children who have been married and on their own for several years say the same thing when they are speaking about us.

We should plan for independence, but avoid obstinacy.

The person, old or young, who makes friends is the one who

listens politely to suggestions, is grateful for them, and accepts and gives credit for those he can use.

Pleasant Companionship

Recently, Mrs. Halsey and I were visiting a small town in Florida with the thought that we might, a little later, wish to live there. We talked with one couple whose home was for sale. The man was honest enough to give me some advice, even though it might lose the sale for him.

He said that, in spite of his being over 65 years old, there was only one man in the whole community younger than he. He and his wife seriously missed not having at least *some* young friends in the neighborhood.

We have discussed this many times since then and have decided that, if we do move, we will select a place where we definitely can have some younger friends as well as friends of our own age.

We have nothing against communities, even homes, designed especially for retired people, and we may yet live in one. But, if we do, we are going to make sure that, close enough to it for us to get there easily, there are churches and groups of all kinds in which there are both young people and old people, each enjoying and profiting from the companionship of the other.

Health

Complete freedom from the aches and pains so often accompanying old age is, of course, not absolutely essential to happiness. We all know people who are so busy thinking of others and trying to give them happiness that their own infirmities seem to be entirely forgotten.

But there is no question but that good health and the ability to be reasonably active physically do make the achievement of happy days after retirement much easier.

And the probability of this condition becoming a reality is greatly increased if we begin to do something about it several years before retirement.

Probably the most important thing is to have regular physical checkups at somewhat more frequent intervals than was necessary when we were younger and to try more carefully than we probably have in the past to follow the doctor's specific instructions to us.

In addition to this there are a few general suggestions:

1. Take regularly some outdoor exercise—something which you enjoy and which is not too strenuous.

2. Do not drive yourself too hard in whatever you are doing. It is not worth the price.

3. Slow down just a little more each year. But when you do this be careful not to make the mistake made by one executive I once knew. He had been urged for some time to delegate some of his responsibilities to a capable younger man in one of his departments. Here are the words he was reported to have used: "Jim, I want you to take full charge of the accounting department, and consult me about everything."

This is a true story. In fact, many years of experience in business organizations leads me to believe that, with just a change in the name of the person and of the department, it is a true story of the majority of "delegations" of responsibility. But this kind of delegation does not keep away the heart attacks suffered by so many executives.

Delegate authority as well as responsibility. *Really turn loose!* It will be good for your health and for the health of the business too.

4. As you grow older, try more and more to avoid situations which might cause worry and tension. For example, if you invest in stocks, change gradually to the more conservative issues.

5. Watch your diet. Too many of us, as we grow older, eat as

much as we did when we were young. An excellent booklet entitled *Food Guide for Older Folks* (Home and Garden Bulletin No. 17) is available from The Superintendent of Documents, Government Printing Office, Washington 25, D.C. Price, 10 cents.

Appreciation and Love

One of the strongest of all emotional hungers is a craving to be appreciated and loved.

This is true of people of all ages, but as we grow older and feel that our powers to do many of the things through which we have gained attention and appreciation are beginning to wane, the hunger grows more and more compelling.

Especially, we worry about the fact that our nieces and nephews and even our children do not seem to love us and to enjoy being with us as much as we think they should.

Older people need love, not pity. They need to have people, old and young, enjoy being with them and talking with them. But we who are growing old sometimes forget that we do not have any real right to expect a full measure of love and appreciation unless we deserve it—*unless we give truly unselfish love and appreciation in return.*

We should never complain about the loneliness of our lives, especially to young people. We should rather encourage them to talk to us about their activities, their accomplishments, and their problems. If we do this regularly, there will soon be no loneliness to complain about.

My mother was bedridden for the last seven years of her life and in almost constant pain. Yet people of all ages came to see her with both their joys and their problems. And, somehow, they always left feeling a little happier.

And she was happy because, in spite of her infirmities, she lived a *useful* life. She was loved and appreciated, not because she demanded love and appreciation as a right, but because she earned it by giving love and appreciation and often real help with their problems to all who came to see her.

All of this should enable us, when we retire, to have a definite feeling of personal worthwhileness and self-respect because we will still be useful, still contributing something to the happiness of those around us.

And that really is the definition of happiness—of happy years after retirement.

Summary

The steps which must be taken to assure a satisfying retirement may be summarized in four words—Planning, Goals, Saving, Initiative.

Planning. Happy years after retirement seldom just happen. Usually there has been planning which started many years before the date of retirement.

Goals. The planning will be much more effective in producing the desired result if definite goals are set, goals which are determined by the specific needs of the person.

Saving. Regular saving should start early and be maintained consistently through the years.

Initiative. A few years before the retirement date, definite steps should be taken to decide upon, to locate, and, if possible, to try out on a part-time basis two or three occupations. And, finally, to determine upon and prepare for the one in every way the best suited to the person.

Suggested Additional Reading on How to Plan for Happy Years After Retirement

The Retirement Handbook by Joseph C. Buckley (New York: Harper & Brothers, Revised 1956):

There is detailed and specific advice and information on practically every aspect of retirement.

The important question of where to live is discussed in considerable detail. The advantages offered by specific cities located in California, Florida, Georgia, South Carolina, North Carolina, the Gulf Coast country and the Southwest are described.

There is an especially good chapter on "A Small Business of Your Own." This includes an unusually comprehensive bibliography of books and trade papers relating to various businesses suitable for retired persons.

These Harvest Years edited by Janet Baird (New York: Doubleday & Company, Inc., 1951):

This book was prepared by a panel of 12 experts, specialists in their fields. Two chapters of special interest are:

> "How to Reach the Harvest Years" by Ernest P. Boas, M.D., which gives specific suggestions on health to the person approaching retirement age.
>
> "How to Keep the Mind Limber" by O. Spurgeon English, M.D., which discusses the often neglected things the older person must do if he wishes to get along well with young people and always to be a welcome guest in *any* age group.

How to Earn an Income While Retired by Norman D. Ford (Greenlawn, New York: Harrian Publications, 1955):

Lists and describes briefly the possibilities of 106 occupations, and gives many general suggestions of value.

And there is an especially interesting chapter on how to make a hobby pay. A list of 140 markets for home crafts and products is included.

One chapter describes the possibilities of ten occupations suitable for invalids.

13

A SUGGESTED PROGRAM FOR BUILDING YOUR OWN SUCCESS

THIS IS THE MOST IMPORTANT CHAPTER IN THE BOOK.

The chapters preceding this have suggested various personal qualities, techniques, and underlying principles as being essential to the achievement of the happiness-building success we all so strongly desire.

And I know that the suggestions offered are sound and practical, because I have seen them produce results time and time again.

But I know, too, how difficult it is to follow persistently any program of self-improvement which lasts over a considerable period of time, no matter how fully convinced we may be of its value. There are so many other things that demand our attention —important things, things often requiring *immediate* attention. So our program is postponed, temporarily, of course. But, unfortunately, it often takes only a few "temporary" postponements to cause the program to be forgotten, unless effective safeguards are provided to prevent this.

For success in carrying out any program for self-improvement there must be two things *in addition to a strong and earnest desire for success.*

First, there must be a definite and carefully laid-out program which is not too complicated and which requires some attention at reasonably regular intervals, but which is not too continuously time-consuming. And it must be so planned that it will continue to be interesting and helpful over a rather long period of time, possibly even several years.

Second, there must be a reasonably automatic system which will remind us again and again of our resolution to carry out the program, and remind us specifically of what we are supposed to do.

A Suggested Program

First, prepare on a letter-size sheet of paper a chart like that shown on page 194.

Second, review the two or three chapters which discuss those things in which you believe you need the most improvement and put your general rating on each of these chapters in the space provided.

Third, in the space to the left of each general rating, write two or three (not over three) of the qualities or techniques discussed in that chapter on which you gave yourself the lowest rating, and the rating you gave yourself on each of these. For chapters which have no self rating, decide on a general rating, and list and rate the two or three things most in need of attention.

Fourth, in about two or three weeks (set a definite date) review the ratings and see if you have made improvement enough to justify increasing any of the ratings and possibly the general rating. Repeat this about each two or three weeks until you feel that your improvement is reasonably permanent. Perhaps you will wish to work on other qualities discussed in these chapters.

POINTS TO BE STRESSED	Your Over-all Rating
Goals	
Personal Qualities	
Worry	
Understanding Behavior	
Friends	
Cooperation from Employees	
Efficiency	
Disappointments	
Letters	
Reports	
Public Speaking	
Retirement	

Fifth, when you feel reasonably satisfied with progress on these chapters, do the same thing for two or three additional chapters, but do not remove your ratings on the other chapters. You will want to come back to them.

Sixth, continue doing this until you cover all of the chapters.

Seventh, after a time, you will probably wish to start over, emphasizing qualities with which you seem to have the most trouble.

A Persistent Reminder

First, you want to be reminded frequently and persistently of the individual qualities or techniques you are working on during the current period.

Second, you want to be reminded of the date on which you plan to review your progress, and to be reminded every day, possibly several times a day, if you have let the date go by.

In my own program, and I have been working on it for several years, I accomplish this by fastening a small card in a conspicuous place in a desk drawer which I open many times each day; on the card I have written the specific things I am working on and the date of the next review. For example the card now looks like this:

Thoroughness
Patience
Little things
Names
April 25

I do not put the ratings on this card. These should always be kept confidential.

Self-improvement is a continuous, never-ending effort, but no other investment will pay bigger dividends in success and happiness.

The Final Responsibility Is Yours

Finally, you must remember that the responsibility for your success or failure is primarily your own. As one chief executive said at a meeting of a group of his supervisors who had been discussing problems of personnel supervision:

"Training is a signpost. It says that this or that is the right road, but you must walk the road yourself."

INDEX

H

I

J

L

M

N

O

P

Q

HOW TO ACHIEVE SUCCESS AND HAPPINESS IN BUSINESS

by GEORGE D. HALSEY

YOU CAN USE this simple, straightforward Success-Plan to win success in your work—happiness in your private life—because this System gives you that "extra something" that makes for success.

YOU WILL FIND this success-winning technique a foolproof way to success and good fortune. It cultivates within you the success-building attributes of Good Judgment, Clear Decision, Cool Poise, Smooth Tact, Wise Leadership—it gives you the "inside" grasp of affairs that lies behind every successful executive.

YOU WOULD HAVE to search out these facts and systems over slow, painful, expensive years of trial-and-error, if George Halsey had not written this book.

YOU WILL DISCOVER here a fresh, exciting new technique which makes it fully possible for you to literally "make your own opportunities," instead of just waiting for them to happen! This powerful technique gives you the self-confidence and enthusiasm you need to leap over the hurdles and go up the ranks much quicker and easier than the other people in your office, who are also competing for the choice promotions and raises.

WHEN YOU FOLLOW this simple, practical Guide to Success you will discover how to get more fun and excitement out of your job, no matter how routine or how boring it may seem to you right now. You will see how to develop new ease in dealing with others, new tact and diplomacy in handling "touchy" or "difficult" individuals, and new ways to win the support, interest and friendship of the people who really count.